COLUMBIA

AN ILLUSTRATED HISTORY

Alan Hawig
June. 1985

FROM SOUTHERN VILLAGE TO MIDWESTERN CITY

COLUMBIA
AN ILLUSTRATED HISTORY

ALAN R. HAVIG

"PARTNERS IN PROGRESS" BY CHRISTOPH SZECHENYI

PUBLISHED IN COOPERATION WITH THE COLUMBIA CHAMBER OF COMMERCE

WINDSOR PUBLICATIONS, INC.
WOODLAND HILLS, CALIFORNIA

THIS BOOK IS DEDICATED TO THE GENERATIONS OF
COLUMBIANS WHO CREATED THEIR CITY'S
FASCINATING HISTORY, AND TO THE GENERATIONS
UNBORN WHO HAVE YET TO BUILD UPON OUR
COMMON PAST.
IT IS DEDICATED ESPECIALLY TO TWO CURRENT
HISTORY-MAKERS, BETTINA AND KIRSTEN, WITH LOVE.

Windsor Publications, Inc.
History Book Division
Publisher: John M. Phillips
Staff for *From Southern Village to Midwestern City: Columbia, An Illustrated History*
Editor and Picture Editor: Laurel H. Paley
Editorial Director, Corporate Biographies: Karen Story
Design Director: Alexander D'Anca
Assistant Director, Corporate Biographies: Phyllis Gray
Editor, Corporate Biographies: Judith Hunter
Editorial Assistants: Patricia Buzard, Lonnie Pham, Pat Pittman
Composing: E. Beryl Myers, Barbara Neiman
Proofreading: Doris R. Malkin
Layout Artist: Chris McKibbin
Production Artist: Lynn Agosti
Marketing Director: Ellen Kettenbeil
Sales Manager: Bob Moffitt
Sales Coordinator: Joan Baker
Sales Representative: Irene Isenburg

Library of Congress Cataloging in Publication Data

Havig, Alan R., 1940-
   From southern village to midwestern city.

   " 'Partners in progress' by Christoph Szechenyi."
   "Published in cooperation with the Columbia Chamber
of Commerce."
   Bibliography: p.
   Includes index.
   1. Columbia (Mo.)—History. 2. Columbia (Mo.)—
Description. 3. Columbia (Mo.)—Industries. I. Title.
F474.C72H38 1984   977.8'29   84-15294
ISBN 0-89781-138-0

Endpapers: Stephens College students pose on a Columbia firetruck in the early 1920s. Courtesy, Stephens College Archives.

Page two: Broadway, Columbia's major thoroughfare, is seen in the early 1930s. Courtesy, National Archives Trust Fund Board

Page six: The old fairgrounds on Wilkes Boulevard featured a half-mile track, and in the early 20th century the annual horse races attracted throngs larger than Columbia's population. From Columbia: The Coming City of Central Missouri, 1910. Courtesy, Carol Crabb

CONTENTS

ACKNOWLEDGMENTS

Many people assisted in the preparation of this book, and I take pleasure in thanking them: James W. Goodrich, Mary K. Dains, and Karen Quiring of the State Historical Society of Missouri; June Dodd, David Duffy, and others connected with the Columbia Chamber of Commerce; Nancy Lankford, Daryl Garwood, and other staff members of the Joint Collection University of Missouri, Western Historical Manuscript Collection-Columbia, State Historical Society of Missouri Manuscripts; D.J. Wade and Clara Williamson of the University of Missouri Archives; President Patsy Sampson of Stephens College and Marguerite Mitchell of the Hugh Stephens Library at Stephens College; Sally Gallion of Columbia College's Office of Public Relations; Christopher L. Mallory of the Columbia Public Schools; Henry Waters III and Francis Pike of the *Columbia Daily Tribune;* Bob Humphries of the *Columbia Missourian;* and Patsy Moore and Michael Kelpe of Boone Hospital Center. I would also like to acknowledge Janice Kahalley (Gottesfeld), Charles Brown, Elizabeth Kennedy, Virginia Botts, Carol Crabb, Sidney Neate, Queen Smith, Mr. and Mrs. Lud Balsamo, Frank Balsamo, Jr., Larry Balsamo, Garland Russell, Wynna Faye Elbert, Mary Brady Biggs, Professor LeRoy Day, Bill Bower, and Al Germond. All students of Columbia's history owe a debt of gratitude to John C. Crighton, whose extensive research and numerous writings are indispensable to an understanding of the city's development.

HISTORY BOOK ADVISORY COMMITTEE

Hartley G. Banks, Jr.; Andrew J. Bass; Virginia Mullinax Botts, Historian and Genealogist; The Honorable Frank Conley, Boone County Circuit Court; Charles Digges, Sr., The Insurance Group; Jack Estes, Central Office Equipment Company; James W. Goodrich, State Historical Society of Missouri; Howard B. Lang, Jr.; Sidney B. Neate; B.D. Simon, B.D. Simon Construction Company; Henry J. Waters III, *Columbia Daily Tribune;* Senator Roger Wilson, Missouri State Senator

CHAPTER ONE
The People

Until treaties abolished the Indians' claims in 1815, Osage and Missouri tribes roamed the land north of the Missouri River. Apparently Native American villages did not stand on the site upon which Columbia would grow, a plateau rising between the two creeks which later settlers would name Flat Branch and Hinkson. Prior to the town's settlement, white explorers passed nearby. The Lewis and Clark expedition pushed its way up the Missouri River to a location 10 miles short of Columbia in 1803. Members of the Daniel Boone family passed to the north of Columbia's location in 1806, on their way to the salt licks of present-day Howard County. Columbia's location, north of the Ozark Plateau and at the southeastern edge of the great prairies stretching north and west, lay quietly unoccupied until the Kentuckians arrived in 1819.

Following the end of the second war with Great Britain in 1815, the Boon's Lick country became a mecca for settlers from the upper South. Located along the Missouri River, 100 miles and more beyond St. Louis, the Boon's Lick became the second area of Missouri to be settled and the most westerly of American frontier settlements. Men who sought rich farmland, quick profits from real estate speculation, or more gradual returns from town-building, flocked to government land auctions, which were held in the bustling town of Franklin beginning in November 1818. On November 13, 1818, a group of men associated with the Smithton Company purchased a 2,720-acre tract that included the site of Columbia. In the spring of the following year the company's trustees established the town of Smithton at a location approximately one-half mile west of the present Boone County Courthouse. Finding the water supply inadequate, the trustees moved their fledgling village eastward across the Flat Branch in 1821. Named Columbia, the relocated town became the seat of Boone County on April 7 of that year.

Columbia's original settlers are appropriately called the Kentuckians. Migrants from central Kentucky made up about 60 percent of Boone County's and Columbia's initial population, including most of early Columbia's leading families, those whose descendants maintained a prominent place in the community for generations. Transplanted Kentuckians included David Todd, first judge of the Boone County Circuit Court; Dr. William Jewell, who, like Todd, had attended Transylvania University in Lexington, Kentucky; James S. Rollins, who would earn the informal title "Father of the University of Missouri;" David Gordon, a wealthy farmer whose land bordered Columbia on the east; and

Odon Guitar, Union general during the Civil War. Families bearing such names as Cave, Gentry, Harris, and Woods also migrated from central Kentucky.

Substantial planters and successful professionals and businessmen who sought to enhance their wealth in a new land, the pioneers brought the slaves, equipment, cash, and know-how to establish a farm, a store, or a law practice. Under their direction Columbia began functioning immediately as the seat of county government and as a trading center for nearby farms.

Intermarriage among the original settlers' numerous descendants helped these families maintain their prominence in the maturing community. Although the Columbia that has rushed headlong into the modern American present has not always preserved the physical evidence of its southern heritage, traces remain in homes named for Gordons and Conleys, for example, and buildings bearing the names of Boone, Gentry, Hickman, and Guitar.

These white families brought slaves to Columbia, and from these bonded laborers has descended the city's black community—another reminder of the city's southern heritage. Slavery was an integral part of Columbia's life until 1865. Slave auctions occurred on the steps of the 1847 courthouse, and the *Missouri Statesman*, edited by William F. Switzler, often carried the results of slave sales and advertisements placed by those who wished to buy or rent slaves or retrieve runaways. Both the university and Christian College hired slaves from local owners to work as domestics or gardeners. Slaves constructed and maintained Columbia streets, worked in various manufacturing concerns, and practiced skilled trades like carpentry. Charley Boyle, a Columbia blacksmith after the Civil War, learned his trade when he was the slave of carriage maker George Washington Gordon.

After emancipation blacks quickly established their own religious, fraternal, and educational institutions and attempted to gain a meaningful economic foothold in the community. Columbia's freedmen reflected the national pattern, however, as most found it impossible to become anything but servants and laborers. An exception is the family of John Lang. Lang, a free black, came to Columbia in 1850 to be near his wife Louisa and children, who were the slaves of the new university president James Shannon. Lang successfully operated a butcher shop in which he employed his slave son, John Jr. Before his death in 1879, John Lang, Sr. also ran a dairy and grocery store, owned considerable real estate, and helped establish black schools and churches. One of his 16 children, Eugenia, married pianist John W. "Blind" Boone. Cynthia, another daughter, taught in the Cummings Academy after the Civil War.

Into the society established by Columbia residents of Southern background came members of other groups, including "Yankees" from states north of the Ohio River. Columbia's educational institutions brought many of them, such as the first university president John Hiram Lathrop, a

Top far left: Missouri honored the recently-deceased Daniel Boone by naming a new county after him in 1820. A resident of Missouri since 1799 when the Spanish controlled it, Boone came to symbolize the pioneer spirit soon displayed by other Kentuckians who migrated to the Boon's Lick country. This engraving appeared on a Missouri state bond in 1837. SHSM

Top center: Dr. William Jewell was one of Columbia's most versatile early setters. In addition to practicing medicine, Jewell served in Columbia city government and the state legislature, speculated in land, designed the 1847 Boone County Courthouse, endowed William Jewell College in Liberty, Missouri, and helped to direct the Columbia Female Academy. SHSM

Top right: Marshall Gordon's great-grandfather David settled near Columbia about 1822; his grandfather John B. served in the legislature from 1830-1840; and his father Boyle built the home known as the "Capen House." Marshall (pictured) provided continuity between Columbia's oldest families and later arrivals like his friend Walter Williams, founder of the university's School of Journalism. From Walter Williams, A History of Northeast Missouri volume II, 1913

Bottom: Fifty years after Columbia's founding, some well-established sons of Kentucky pioneers commissioned St. Louis architects to design their houses. The home of Robert L. Prewitt, built in 1871 at Price and Broadway, was one of many residences which symbolized the solid economic and social position of Columbia's second and third generation descendants of the original settler group. SHSM

Catch the Runaway!

RANAWAY from the subscriber, living in Columbia, Mo., on the night of the 26th inst., a mulatto man named **Charles**, about twenty-six years old, near six feet high; will weigh about 180 pounds; wears his hair long and in plaits. He has plenty of the best clothing, but I don't know what kind he wore away. He has a fine gold watch and plenty of money, and will doubtless try to get a pass. He is a blacksmith by trade.

For his apprehension in Boone county I will pay a reward of $25; in any adjoining county $50; in any other county or out of the State $100—these sums being designed to include the reward fixed by law.

April 28, 1854.   **GEO. W. GORDON.**

Above: Alexander Stewart, a native of Paisley, Scotland, established a painting and wallpapering business upon his arrival in Columbia in 1878. In 1890 the 45-year-old Stewart traveled to Paisley to get married. Returning to Columbia with his wife Jeanie, Stewart found an abundance of work in Columbia's early 20th century building boom. From Columbia Missouri Herald, 25th Anniversary Historical Edition, 1895

Above left: One of Columbia's late 19th century Yankees was Iowan O.H. Tiede. Trained in Chicago and Germany, Tiede taught music at Christian College from 1887 to 1893. For a few years during the 1890s he operated the Columbia College of Music and Oratory, but then closed it and left the city. Columbia's population has always consisted of temporary residents like Tiede and deeply-rooted families like the Gordons. From Columbia Missouri Herald, 25th Anniversary Historical Edition, 1895

Top: John Lang, Jr., like his father, was an entrepreneur. During the 1870s he owned a construction company that did city and county road work and provided jobs for blacks. From 1880 until the end of World War I he managed the concert tours of "Blind" Boone. SHSM

Yale graduate, and Lucy Ann Wales, the first preceptress of the Columbia Female Academy and a native of Massachusetts. After the Civil War two New England natives were deans at the university: George C. Swallow, head of the College of Agriculture, and Erastus L. Ripley, who led the Normal School faculty. By 1895 several leading Columbia merchants were natives of northern states: George F. Troxell of Pennsylvania was an undertaker and furniture retailer; Wisconsin native William B. Nowell operated a grocery store; and Ohioan C.B. Miller owned a shoe store.

Foreign emigration, which reshaped many American localities from the 1840s to the 1920s, had a negligible impact on Columbia. Many Germans immigrated to nearby Missouri counties after 1840, but most remained south of the river and east of Boone County. Less than one percent of Columbia's population was found to be "foreign born white" in the census counts of 1900 through 1930. The foreign-born who did find their way to Columbia often came as university faculty members or to other professional employment: they did not constitute a labor force for contractors or manufacturers. For example, Canadian John Davison Lawson was professor of law in the 1890s, the decade that the Reverend Patrick Francis O'Reilly, an Irish priest, served the Sacred Heart parish. Immigrants joined the business community as well. Frederick Bihr, for example, arrived from Germany in 1865 to build wagons. Several businesses owned by Chinese immigrants, including the Yee Sing Laundry, operated during the 1920s. In recent years Southeast Asian immigrants have contributed to the city's ethnic diversity, as have university faculty members and students from non-Western nations.

Columbia's population has also included college students, that transient group upon which so much of the community's identity and economic health depends. If Yankees and immigrants made the southern village more diverse and cosmopolitan, so too did the students. During Christian Female College's first year, 1851-1852, 31 of 70 students were from other Missouri towns and five were from out of state. In 1903-1904 students from Argentina, Canada, China, Cuba, Egypt, Mexico, Japan, and Trinidad attended the university. From the days of crowded railroad depots to today's jammed dormitory parking lots, the regular coming and going of students have been an important factor in the ebb and flow of the community's life.

Young and old; black and white; Yankee and southerner; native and foreign—how did these population groups interrelate? Like every community, Columbia has experienced divisiveness. Some potential lines of conflict have been relatively unimportant. Few expressions of nativism appeared in a place with so few foreign-born permanent residents. Also, in a town whose population is one-third students, serious incidents among or by students—such as the 1853 murder of B.F. Handy by fellow student W.W. Thornton in the east corridor of Academic Hall—have been unusual. Since 1841, when the university began operations, the town-

Above: Following the example of his uncle Moses (a Rocheport merchant), Victor Barth left Germany for central Missouri at the end of the Civil War. With his brother Joseph, Victor operated a clothing and dry goods store in Columbia from 1868 until 1909. Columbia's late 19th century Jewish community included other German-born merchants such as Simon Henry Levy, who owned a shoe store, and Bernhard Loeb, a grocer. From Walter Williams, A History of Northeast Missouri *volume II, 1913*

Opposite page, bottom: The laws governing slavery gave masters near-absolute control, but the slaves' own actions constantly compromised white power. Slaves feigned illness, ran away, murdered their masters, and in countless other ways helped to shape the institution. As this 1854 newspaper advertisement in the Weekly Missouri Statesman *reveals, Charley Boyle risked much for his freedom, years before the Civil War ended slavery. SHSM*

Above: Early in the 20th century Stephens College students from other states maintained their home-state identity by forming clubs. Pictured is the Oklahoma Club in about 1912. Courtesy, Stephens College Archives

Right: The identity of this man and child is unknown. The photographer, a Stephens College student enrolled in a contemporary issues course in the mid-1950s, left the classroom to study local housing conditions. Those who teach and learn at Columbia's three colleges have long used the city as a laboratory, thus creating a unique interaction among Columbia's population groups. Courtesy, Social Sciences-History Department, Stephens College

Left: In September 1914 students renew an annual ritual as they arrive on a Wabash train for the start of a new school year. From the A.M. Finley Photograph Albums, volume II. Courtesy, Joint Collection University of Missouri, Western Historical Manuscript Collection-Columbia, State Historical Society of Missouri Manuscripts

Below left: Around 1910 the F.W. Quinn family posed for this portrait on the steps of their home on Sixth Street. For some Columbians between the Civil War and World War I, the "extended family" included not only members of several generations but also servants. Black domestics rarely appear in photos of white families. SHSM

Below far left: Some Columbians left only their images as documents for later generations to ponder. Was child care an unfamiliar responsibility for this young father? Was he sobered by the news from Europe, where war began during the year this photo was taken (1914)? The child, perhaps, lived to experience the next great war less than 30 years later. From the A.M. Finley Photograph Albums, volume I. Courtesy, Joint Collection University of Missouri, Western Historical Manuscript Collection-Columbia, State Historical Society of Missouri Manuscripts

gown relationship has been exceptionally positive and constructive. Although the noted economist and social theorist Thorstein Veblen characterized Columbia as "a woodpecker hole of a town in a rotten stump called Missouri," most college faculty members have become more successfully integrated into the community.

More serious inter-group conflict resulted from slavery and racial prejudice, generating violence in Columbia as it did elsewhere. Perhaps the most tragic such incident, if only because it is the most recent, was the lynching of James T. Scott in 1923. The 14-year-old daughter of a university professor had identified Scott, a janitor employed by the school, as the man who had attempted to molest her near Stewart's Bridge. Between 11 p.m. and midnight on Saturday, April 28, as law officers stood by, a mob of around 500 townspeople and students pushed and dragged Scott along the mile-long route to the scene of the alleged crime and hanged him from the bridge—which ironically led to beautiful suburban developments, a symbol of community progress for many white Columbians. Not since the Civil War had Columbia's southern orientation been so starkly revealed, this time for the nation to witness.

Blacks, since 1890, have constituted a steadily shrinking proportion of Columbia's population. In 1890, a quarter of a century after emancipation, blacks added up to nearly 40 percent of the 4,000 Columbians counted in the census. By 1920 the black community amounted to 18.47 percent of the total population, and by 1950 the percentage had declined to 7.9. Throughout these years, however, blacks made up a larger proportion of Columbia's population than they did that of Missouri as a whole, a reminder that Boone County was one of the state's leading slaveholding counties during the antebellum period.

Having grown in population from 651 (in 1850) to 62,061 (at the most recent census), today Columbia is the largest city in the central part of Missouri, although it only recently gained that distinction. Jefferson City, the location of state government which also benefited from Missouri River traffic and mainline railroad service, was larger than Columbia until the 1940s. Not until 1900 did Columbia's population surpass that of Mexico in neighboring Audrain County. Until the same date Fulton and Columbia were of approximately equal size. The history of central Missouri's towns includes one-and-one-half centuries of competition for public institutions and private businesses, and Columbia's population growth reflects its considerable success in obtaining them.

On the eve of its centennial, in the decade which followed 1910, Columbia was a bustling and diverse community. Faculty homes and student rooming houses surrounded the university campus in the south part of town. Nationally recognized scholars pursued their research amid the swirl of student academic and social life. While in Columbia, Thorstein Veblen wrote *The Instinct of Workmanship and the State of the Industrial Arts* (1914), a volume which he later claimed was his only

Columbia's residential areas grew to the north, east, and south of the original town, a space bounded by today's Park Avenue, Hitt and Elm streets, and the cemetery road east of the present Garth Avenue. The town's most attractive, prestigious 19th-century neighborhoods developed east of the business district. Oliver Parker's home (pictured below, SHSM) was photographed in the late 1860s after it had been purchased by Stephens College. Many showpiece homes, including that of the Charles B. Bowling family (pictured below right, from Columbia: The Coming City of Central Missouri, 1910. Courtesy, Carol Crabb), have been tragically destroyed by fire. A 1907 postcard shows turn-of-the-century College Avenue (pictured right, SHSM, gift of Trenton Boyd).

Below right: The fairgrounds attracted large crowds to the north part of Columbia for a week of fun each summer in the early 20th century. The midway, shown here circa 1910, was located north of the intersection of Wilkes Boulevard and Washington Street, on the present Hickman High School grounds. From Columbia: The Coming City of Central Missouri, 1910. Courtesy, Carol Crabb

Below: This 1908 view of Waugh Street near Locust shows a typical street in older parts of Columbia. The Columbia Theater billboard behind Lee School advertised a Western adventure that evening—for a nickel. Courtesy, Horticultural Department, University of Missouri-Columbia, and State Historical Society of Missouri

Above: As children played behind the Jefferson School at Eighth and Rogers streets on March 12, 1908, the camera captured a rare glimpse of the nearby neighborhood north of the business district. Cities like Columbia, proud of recent growth, preferred to impress visitors and potential residents with views of finer residential districts and business and public buildings. Courtesy, Horticultural Department, University of Missouri-Columbia, and State Historical Society of Missouri

important book. East of the retail district lay Columbia's most attractive and prestigious residential neighborhood at the turn of the century. But Judge John A. Stewart's development, Westmount and Westwood, would soon claim that distinction.

Also adjacent to the business district was Columbia's largest black neighborhood. Extending from the Katy tracks and Cemetery Hill north beyond Park Avenue, and from the area behind the courthouse west to First Street, the community contained the Douglass School, several churches, and a scattering of black businesses. A neighborhood feature condemned by both Columbians and visitors was Flat Branch. The picturesque creek of earlier days had become an open sewer which flowed near homes from Switzler Street south past the Missouri, Kansas & Texas (MK&T) depot. A smaller black neighborhood stretched to the northeast along Railroad Street, which paralleled the Wabash.

By the early 20th century Columbia had firmly established its identity as a city of professionals and white collar workers. Nevertheless there was a working class district, located in the northern part of the city. Here in modest housing lived the families of the carpenters, plasterers and others employed in the construction industry; the teamsters, clerks, and unskilled laborers who walked to jobs in the retail section; and the male and female operatives who labored in the Hamilton-Brown Shoe Company factory at Wilkes Boulevard and Fay Street. The few retail stores that served the north end grew in number beginning in the 1920s, when highways 63 and 40 attracted roadside businesses. Columbia's high school also stood in the north part of town, at Eighth and Rogers streets.

A century after its founding, the southern village of the 1820s had become a much more complex and diverse community than its founders could have imagined, and late 20th century Columbia would amaze those who experienced the city around 1920. The pages and pictures which follow will suggest the broad outlines of change in the political, economic, educational, cultural, and religious life as Columbia grew from village to city.

CHAPTER TWO
The Public Life

James Sidney Rollins was perhaps Columbia's most important political figure from the mid-1830s until his death. His greatest service was, first, to the University of Missouri, which as legislator and curator he founded and guided, and second, to the cause of the Union. As a conservative Unionist congressman from a war-wracked border district, Rollins earned the gratitude of President Lincoln. He is pictured here with his five sons. SHSM, gift of Ruth Rollins Westphal

No public event in Columbia's history has had more profound consequences than the Civil War. Southerners, unlike most other Americans, have suffered from a war fought in their own communities, and Columbians were border-state Southerners in 1861. Although no "official" battles occurred in Columbia, city residents shared with other Missourians the shattering experiences of military occupation, family division, and guerrilla warfare. This conflict—which split the white community, freed hundreds of slaves, disrupted the local economy, halted education, and determined the town's politics for a century—surpasses in importance all other crises which Columbia has faced.

From 1836 to 1854, when the Whigs were one of America's two major political parties, Boone was Missouri's "Banner Whig County." However, the slavery issue proved a dilemma to the Whigs. They shared their party's belief in a strong national government, that could control the nation's banks and develop a transportation system. But a powerful government could also interfere with slavery and prevent its spread into new territories. While abolitionist northern Whigs, who later became Republicans, advocated just such a program, southern party members defended and profited from slavery.

The ties which uneasily bound many Columbians to the Union in 1861 had numerous origins, one of which was service in earlier American wars. Many men who later supported the Union cause, such as Odon Guitar and James S. Rollins, fought in the Black Hawk Indian War of 1832, the Seminole Indian War in 1837, or the Mexican War of 1846-1848. One of Columbia's founders, tavernkeeper Richard Gentry, led the First Regiment of Missouri Volunteers against the Seminoles in Florida and died in that engagement. During the Mexican War a company of local men called the Boone Guards served with Colonel Sterling Price's mounted regiment in Santa Fe, and a few soldiers from the unit fought further south under Colonel Alexander Doniphan.

In the critical years from 1854 to 1861 when the Whig party's demise seemed to foretell the nation's dissolution, many Columbians agonized over the search for a new political home. The majority, prior to the war's outbreak, rejected what they saw as extremism: voters gave Abraham Lincoln only 12 votes in 1860 and refused the appeals of Southern nationalists as well. Through their votes in the late 1850s and in 1860, Columbians endorsed compromise and nationalism, hoping for a solution that would guarantee southern rights and protect slavery, but also preserve

Above: William C. "Bloody Bill" Anderson was one of the Confederate irregulars who perfected guerrilla tactics a century before the Vietnam War. Seen as a Robin Hood figure by sympathizers, Anderson is judged a psychopathic murderer by modern historians. Jesse James rode with Anderson. SHSM

Top: William Franklin Switzler, respected journalist and political partisan, is shown at right in this informal portrait with his brother Lewis. First a Whig and then a Democrat, his public service included three terms in the state legislature, membership in the Missouri Constitutional Conventions of 1865 and 1875, and appointment as chief of the Bureau of Statistics in the U.S. Treasury Department. SHSM

the Union. The firing on Fort Sumter and Lincoln's call to arms in April 1861 forced Columbians finally to choose sides. Mass meetings dramatized the division of this village which had material and intangible ties to both the Confederacy and the Union. A Southern Rights meeting held at the courthouse on April 20, 1861, reminded Columbians of their roots in the South, cheered Jefferson Davis and the Confederate flag, and called for Missouri's secession from the United States. An even larger Union meeting convened at the courthouse on May 6. Some slaveholders who attended this rally hoped that loyalty to the national government was slavery's surest protection; others placed the nation above all else. James S. Rollins expressed this attitude in 1862: "My motto is 'save the nation at any cost'. . . . In regard to African slavery, I value far higher the permanency of the Government and preservation of the Constitution—for these are essential to our liberties."

Through the end of 1861 Union forces largely ignored Columbia as they sought to control rail and river routes to the north and south. Local residents with Southern sympathies freely joined General Sterling Price's state milita; by early October the group included a regiment of Boone County men. County Sheriff John M. Samuel and a company calling itself the Columbia Greys joined Price's force in the Battle of Boonville on June 17, 1861. During the fall of that year Confederate military units passed through Columbia and nearby rural communities, pillaging the area and spreading fear. Twice that fall detachments of Union forces briefly appeared in Columbia to assert federal authority, but to no avail. On December 20, 1861, guerrillas sabotaged a 50-mile stretch of the North Missouri Railroad northeast of Columbia, and eight days later the Mount Zion Methodist Church, 10 miles from town, was the scene of a brief battle. Events had demonstrated that Columbia and Boone County were not safely under Union control. To secure the area Colonel Lewis Merrill's Second Cavalry regiment, Missouri Volunteers, occupied Columbia on January 2, 1862. Establishing their camp on the university grounds, the unit remained for six months. For the remainder of the war, federal troops occupied the town.

One mission of these forces was to suppress outlaw guerrilla bands. On occasion the militiamen acted ruthlessly, as when they summarily executed local citizens Martin E. Oldham and Major William Cave as Southern sympathizers. Union forces also aggravated relations with the local citizenry by rigorously enforcing the loyalty oath required of civil officials by the state. The military required even university faculty members to pledge that they had not supported the Southern cause. On February 8, 1862, Colonel Merrill removed from office four members of the Columbia Board of Trustees because some had refused to take the oath. In April defiant Columbia voters returned the board members to office.

Columbia's occupation by Union forces did not deter Confederate sympathizers or establish order. On August 13, 1862, for example,

Left: General Richard Gentry's death in battle led to a unique career for his widow, Ann Hawkins Gentry. Richard Gentry was Columbia's second postmaster. Ann became its third in 1838, when Senator Thomas Hart Benton overcame President Martin Van Buren's doubts about "the legality of appointing a lady" to the position. The second woman "postmaster" in American history, Ann resigned in 1865. She was the mother of 13 children. SHSM, gift of Mary Paxton Keeley

Above: The national media gave extensive coverage to one of the most striking events of the Civil War: the induction of former slaves into the Union Army. This illustration entitled "Negro Recruits Boarding Train" appeared in Frank Leslie's Illustrated Newspaper on May 7, 1864. The army and the Freedmen's Bureau helped some blacks begin the difficult but exhilarating transition from slavery to freedom. SHSM

Southern partisan Henry Martyn Cheavens saw action with Confederate forces in the Deep South as well as in Missouri. Ironically, he was a northerner who was born in Philadelphia, educated at Yale and Amherst, and employed in Illinois. Cheavens lived in rural Boone County for more than a half-century after the Civil War, practicing two professions, medicine and teaching. SHSM, gift of Virginia Easley

Below: Luella St. Clair-Moss is one of three Missouri women placed on the League of Women Voters' National Roll of Honor. A firm but diplomatic suffrage advocate, she soothed the fears of Congressman William L. Nelson in April 1919. He worried about the "unbecoming attitude" of radical feminists in Washington. She thought it "hardly fair to stigmatize several million women for what a few over-zealous ones did" in the nation's Capital. Courtesy, Columbia Chamber of Commerce

Above: President Harry Truman, Missouri's number one Democrat, received an honorary degree from his home state's university on June 9, 1950. The photograph shows Truman—standing to the left of Dr. Frederick Middlebush, university president—greeting other guests in Jesse Hall. The Chief Executive's address to the graduates, delivered shortly before the Korean War began, called for continued American economic aid to Western Europe. Courtesy, University of Missouri Archives

Left: One of the most popular speakers in an era which valued oratory, William Jennings Bryan toured America even when he was not campaigning for office. Here he is pictured addressing a Chautauqua crowd at Maysville in the early 20th century—a scene nearly identical to Chautauquas in Columbia. A local Chautauqua, which mixed popular education and entertainment, provided valuable exposure and a good summer income to perennial candidates like Bryan. SHSM

100 guerrillas led by Young Purcell rode into town to free Confederates from jail. One of the raiders, Boone Countian Henry Martyn Cheavens, later wrote of the incident:

(We) entered Columbia about 1 p.m. with a whoop and a yell, clattering over the ground rough shod down to the Court House door. The Federals all ran to the University, scattering in all directions. Our men went to work breaking down the jail door and releasing the prisoners, who were led off in triumph.

The guerrillas left town with 100 head of government horses and a souvenir U.S. flag, scraps of which were later sewn into quilts. Columbians improved the fortifications at the courthouse and the university's Academic Hall. But well into 1864 they saw evidence of their vulnerability. One chilling reminder was Bloody Bill Anderson's massacre of over 100 federal troops at Centralia in northern Boone County on September 27, 1864. Panic swept through Columbia as a result of Anderson's raids and the approach from the south of General Price's 12,000-man invasion force in early October. Local citizens, including leading businessmen, organized the Columbia Tigers, a defense force, and built a blockhouse at Eighth and Broadway. However, when Price lost and Anderson died at the Battle of Westport (near present-day Kansas City) on October 23, 1864, Columbians could believe that the worst was over.

Columbians both white and black served the Union cause, although often in non-combatant roles. James S. Rollins represented Missouri's ninth district in Congress from 1861 to 1865. William F. Switzler assumed the post of provost marshal for the ninth congressional district in July 1863. And Odon Guitar, who organized the Ninth Cavalry Regiment of the Missouri State Militia in central Missouri counties in 1863, commanded that detachment until 1864, retiring to his Columbia law practice with the rank of brigadier general. Slaves, too, joined the Union forces. As early as February 1862 a few slaves escaped bondage by joining a large troop of federal infantry which passed through Columbia. By 1863 the sanctions which had supported the slave system had ceased to operate, and blacks emancipated themselves simply by leaving their owners. Many blacks traveled to St. Louis by way of Jefferson City for service in the army, and beginning in January 1864 black volunteers enlisted in Columbia. One out of every five black males in Boone County served the Union military cause, a total of about 500 former slaves.

The Civil War caused a political transformation in Columbia and Boone County. While in northern states many former Whigs emerged from the war as Republicans, in the South most became Democrats. Columbia, as it did so often, duplicated the southern pattern. There were exceptions. Odon Guitar helped lead local Republicans until his death in 1908, and James S. Rollins eventually supported the G.O.P. But most of Columbia's ex-Whigs joined with pre-war Democrats to make that party the dominant

The exuberant grassroots politics that George Caleb Bingham recorded in his four election paintings has a long local history. Bingham's 1854 painting Stump Speaking *depicts a central Missouri campaign practice that the 19th century gave to the 20th: as recently as the early 1970s Boone County Democrats still held "speakings" in Columbia. SHSM*

one for a century, beginning in 1870. Republicans suffered for their sponsorship of emancipation, black voting, and the disfranchisement of Confederates. The highlight of each election year became the Democratic "speaking," a series of rallies held throughout the county, addressed by those seeking office in the party. William Jennings Bryan, three-time Presidential candidate, most accurately reflected local Democratic beliefs and generated the most intense voter loyalty. Bryan spoke to large Columbia crowds in 1896, 1906, and 1918. Between 1872 and 1964, Democratic candidates like Bryan carried Boone County in every Presidential election.

Columbia's and Boone County's reliable Democratic majorities assisted Missouri's first woman congressional nominee, Luella W. St. Clair-Moss. Moss, who was the president-emeritus of Christian College, ran for the eighth district seat in 1922. Expecting to draw support from recently-enfranchised female voters, she mixed traditional Democratic appeals with less familiar ones: "The woman voter with half of the voting strength can make this government . . . what she wills it to be." Moss won the August primary, a 2,000-vote plurality in Boone County giving her the edge over two male opponents. But in November Republican Sidney C. Roach won the House seat.

As the names Gentry and Guitar suggest, Columbia's Republicans were a respected minority even though they failed to make a respectable showing at the polls. North Todd Gentry, who served as Missouri's attorney general from 1925 to 1928 represents many Republicans who contributed to their party's success statewide. Republicans began cutting into Democratic majorities following Harry Truman's retirement from the Presidency. Dwight D. Eisenhower in 1952 and 1956 won 10 percent more of Boone County's vote than had any previous Republican Presidential candidate. And in three of the four Presidential elections following 1968, Republicans carried the city and county. In 1966 Columbia voters elected their first Republican official when George Parker captured a seat in the legislature. Today the city enjoys the genuine party competition which Whig and Democratic dominance had long made impossible.

While the Civil War divided Columbians, most of America's foreign conflicts since the 1890s have brought them together. Local citizens joined other Americans in denouncing Spanish barbarities in Cuba in 1898, and crowds massed at the Wabash station to cheer departing soldiers. The Spanish-American War not only united white families which had fought on opposing sides in the 1860s, but also gave Columbia's segregated racial groups a common patriotic cause. Dr. J.E. Perry and the Reverend W.T. Osborne organized a company of black soldiers in the spring of 1898. The unit did not see action, but it generated great pride in Columbia's black neighborhood as the "crack company" of the Seventh Regiment, United States Volunteers while in training at Camp Hamilton, Kentucky.

Compared with the trauma of the War between the States, Columbia's experiences of the world wars and Korea were somewhat remote. Scores of men from the community and the university did die in distant places, and others changed their normal routine for overtime hours and civil defense work or made financial sacrifices to buy war bonds. Nevertheless, even during wartime, much about life in Columbia fit comfortable and familiar patterns.

The community's involvement in the First World War—although enthusiastic—points out the remoteness of foreign conflicts after the Civil War. Most Columbians accepted war in 1917. Few had been born in "enemy" nations; Woodrow Wilson, a popular Democrat, directed American diplomacy; and local farmers profited from high wartime prices. Men and women sold Liberty Bonds, raised Red Cross funds, and served on the draft board, the Boone County Council of Defense, and other agencies designed to mobilize effort and opinion. Local citizens donated $20,000 to provide machine shops for army engineer trainees at the university. The town was flooded with students enrolled in war-related programs; some found emergency housing in the Athens Hotel and the Missouri Bible College. Emotionalizing their patriotism, Columbians re-named "Keiser" Avenue for President Wilson and ceased teaching German in the high school.

Wars have not been the only dramatic events of national scope to elicit a response from Columbians. In recent decades the civil rights and women's movements have brought previously excluded groups into a more complete participation in the community's public life.

Lawyers fought the early battles of the civil rights movement, and one important court case challenged segregation at the University of Missouri. In 1939 the United States Supreme Court ordered the law school to enroll Lloyd L. Gaines after declaring unconstitutional Missouri's practice of sending black students to other states for programs not available at Lincoln University in Jefferson City. Also many city residents, especially blacks, lived in deteriorating dwellings. With aid from federal programs, in the 1950s and 1960s Columbia cleared blighted areas and constructed public housing. Encouraged by national events, local blacks and whites acted through churches and civil rights groups like the N.A.A.C.P. to accelerate school desegregation and open public accommodations to all, among other goals. The old ways slowly lost their grip on a city which became visibly less southern. Athletics in the schools, for example, proved to be more than pastimes as black athletes undermined old attitudes through their performance on previously all-white teams. In 1983 a black chief of police, William E. Dye, headed the force which had failed to prevent James T. Scott's death by lynching 60 years earlier.

The national movement for women's equality also found local expression in Columbia, a community that hosted two women's colleges. The Columbia Equal Suffrage Association, organized in November 1912,

Above: In the wake of Pearl Harbor, Columbia spent the summer of 1942 preparing for war. Although far from ocean waters, the university trained many military personnel, including sailors. These men are turning south on 10th Street from Broadway (traffic signals like the one shown functioned for many years on Broadway). Courtesy, University of Missouri Archives

Right: During the Spanish-American War in 1898, many university men enlisted in Company I of the Fifth Missouri Regiment. This photo shows some of them during a break in training. Three student volunteers died in the war; their names appear on a memorial in Jesse Hall. From the F. A. Middlebush papers. Courtesy, Joint Collection University of Missouri, Western Historical Manuscript Collection-Columbia, State Historical Society of Missouri Manuscripts

Six weeks after the Japanese attack on Pearl Harbor, Stephens College students launched a campus campaign to sell $10,000 worth of defense stamps and bonds. A few blocks away, enlistment and the draft decimated the university's male enrollment. America's wars have demanded much of Columbia's student population, and from the Mexican War through Vietnam they have responded with seriousness and responsibility. Courtesy, Stephens College Archives and Wide World Photos

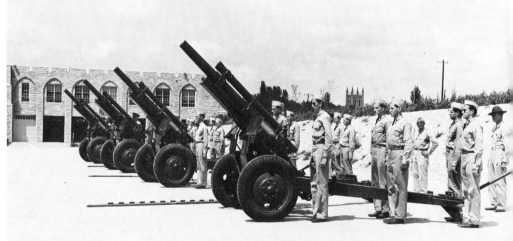

Above: In 1942 Army ROTC cadets trained at the university armory, which was completed in 1940 as a joint project of the state and the Works Projects Administration. The building was named for General Enoch Crowder, a Missouri native who taught military science at the university during the 1880s. Crowder later served as Judge Advocate General of the U.S. Army, administrator of the World War I draft, and ambassador to Cuba during the 1920s. Courtesy, University of Missouri Archives

Above: The frequent appearance of nationally recognized authorities, authors, performers, and public figures makes Columbia an exciting place to live for many of its citizens. New York Congresswoman Shirley Chisholm appeared at a university-sponsored conference in 1967. Courtesy, University of Missouri Archives

Opposite page, bottom: One-half mile due north of the university's Academic Hall in the middle of what had been Eighth Street stood the 1847 Boone County Courthouse. Citizens convened hundreds of meetings in this building to discuss issues of burning interest as well as to celebrate national holidays and civic achievements. From Souvenir of Picturesque Columbia. Courtesy, Stephens College Archives

led the local struggle for women's right to vote. Although the association included men—among them the group's first leader, retired university president Richard H. Jesse—women appropriately supplied most of the energy and commitment. Member Mary Asbury McKay also served as Secretary of the Missouri Suffrage Association, made street speeches in St. Louis, and organized suffrage clubs in southwest Missouri. Association members stumped for equal suffrage at Democratic "speakings" held in Ashland and other county towns in 1914. Rose Russell Ingles was among the Columbia women to testify before legislative hearings on suffrage. University professor Ella Victoria Dobbs paid tribute to the dedication of such women when she recalled her own experiences: "The suffrage movement was a consecration to a cause that was almost a crusade." To further its work the association sponsored educational meetings and welcomed national women's leaders to Columbia, including Jane Addams of Chicago's Hull House. In 1919 the Columbia Equal Suffrage Association became a chapter of the League of Women Voters.

The history of local government also provides insight into Columbia's public life. Since 1821 county politics, the proceedings of the judicial circuit court and administrative county court, and business generated by local lawyers have together constituted an important industry for the city. Three courthouses, constructed on the public square in 1824, 1847, and 1909, have housed this industry. Through at least the first century of Columbia's history, lawyers tended to constitute an interrelated and self-perpetuating group. For example, 13 descendants of pioneer David Gordon became lawyers. Representatives of old families circulated through elective offices, well out of proportion to their numbers in the population, into the 20th century.

A functioning village and a county seat since 1821, Columbia was declared an incorporated town by the county court in November 1826 and thus obtained a state-approved governmental structure. For the next 66 years an elected five-member board of trustees governed Columbia. In 1892 the town adopted a mayor/council form of government. This structure was modified when, in 1949, citizens approved a city manager charter. Although the structure of Columbia's government changed, the city's problems have changed little. The construction and maintenance of streets and the availability and cost of public services and utilities are questions that still confront Columbians into the 1980s. But over the decades the city has gradually assumed greater responsibility for providing facilities and services.

Until late in the 19th century city government supplied few of the services which residents today take for granted. Prompted by the desire to facilitate the downtown retail trade and the wish to impress visitors to the university with Columbia's progressive spirit, citizens made street improvement an early issue. In 1844 Dr. William Jewell won election to the board of trustees on a platform of grading and macadamizing

Above: As these unidentified local suffrage workers planned strategy in 1914, the map on their office wall reminded them of the challenge they faced. Missouri was one of a minority of states, mostly southern, which denied women the vote in all elections. But since suffrage activists tended to be comfortably middle class and well educated, Columbia was a community receptive to their appeals. From the A.M. Finley Photograph Albums, volume I. Courtesy, Joint Collection University of Missouri, Western Historical Manuscript Collection-Columbia, State Historical Society of Missouri Manuscripts

Above left: College students in every era confront serious issues of immediate relevance. At no time has this been more true than during the 1960s and 1970s, when such public issues as civil rights and fighting in Southeast Asia brought student activism to levels not seen since the 1930s. Pictured is a free speech rally called by the university chapter of Students for a Democratic Society in February 1969. Courtesy, University of Missouri Archives

Left: On the day before the 1847 court-house was torn down, county officials gathered one last time beside the columns on the front steps. The inscription above the door at 721 East Walnut, written by Dr. William Jewell, read: "Oh Justice, When Expelled from Other Habitations, Make This Thy Dwelling Place." Wreckers salvaged the inscribed plaque for preservation in the new building. SHSM

Below left: Part of Columbia's fire department at Eighth Street and Park Avenue posed circa 1910. Slow to develop a professional force, the city did not purchase its first horse-drawn fire wagon until 1901 or pay fire fighters until the following year. Columbia purchased its first motorized fire truck in 1913. Well into the 20th century, volunteers were needed to supplement the staff of full-time fire fighters. SHSM

Broadway. Although most residents approved of the plan and praised the results, some objected to increased taxation and complained that merchants alone would benefit. Such reactions have echoed through the years. Responding to pressure from groups like the Commercial Club, which considered paved streets "the crying need of this community," the city paid for a brick surface on Broadway and other streets beginning in 1906. Until the late 19th century Columbia had no sewage system, no municipal water supply (other than several shallow wells in the center of town), no fire department, hospital, or means of refuse collection. Livestock on the one hand increased pollution and on the other hand provided one means of garbage disposal. It was as late as 1917 that the city designated two men as "scavengers" to collect refuse.

A number of factors explain the gradual assumption of public responsibility for community services. The growth of the town in area and numbers made individual solutions to such needs as a water supply and waste disposal less acceptable as time passed. Improved medical knowledge and simple observation convinced many that outhouses were dangerous if located on the banks of Flat Branch or near wells. Technological change also played a part: only a central generating plant could effectively supply electricity to homes and businesses. And finally, crisis and disaster forced change. When the university's Academic Hall burned in January 1892, some state legislators called for the relocation of the institution in another Missouri city since Columbia (they correctly charged) had no fire department worthy of the name. To retain the university the city pledged to build a central water pumping station and locate fire hydrants in the school's neighborhood. The Academic Hall disaster led directly to the establishment of a privately owned Columbia Water and Light Company in 1893 and a municipally owned waterworks and electric generating plant in 1904.

Thus Columbia matured in an age which took citizen participation in community affairs for granted. Early southern settlers brought to Missouri habits of oratory, electioneering, and group organization, which they and their heirs successfully applied to public concerns. As important as the continuing vitality of this tradition is the inclusion of greater numbers of Columbians in the community's common life. That "the public" now includes blacks, women, and youth is one of the most important legacies of Columbia's past.

CHAPTER THREE
The Economic Community

Proud of Columbia's recent growth, a local booster in 1910 predicted a rosy economic future: "there's lots of room for men who want to invest money and roll up their sleeves in the good fight for wholesome, honest dollars." The efforts of local business and civic leaders, beginning in the 19th century, brought key economic institutions to Columbia, including colleges, railroads, industries, and hospitals which together have determined the nature and insured the success of the local economy.

Important to Columbia's growth have been its transportation and communication links to the national economy. Easy and inexpensive access to transportation, in particular, allowed area farmers to market crops, branch factories to function, and organizations to hold conventions in the city. Before the Civil War Columbia enjoyed transportation advantages, which it lost by the 1860s. A business organization's lament in the mid-1950s reflected a long-standing local concern: "Transportation service is still the biggest problem hanging over our heads." Happily Columbia has regained important transportation links, as highways and airways have replaced railroads.

Prior to the Civil War Columbia enjoyed a strategic location on the major trade and travel routes to the West. The Boon's Lick Trail, the main road from St. Louis to Franklin and other Missouri frontier settlements, ran down Broadway beginning in 1822, and 10 miles to the south lay the most important water route to the West, the Missouri River. Before the mid-1850s Columbia benefited from the movement of Americans westward. Settlers in their wagons would pass through the city, stopping to spend money with local outfitters. Also, the annual expedition of Santa Fe traders might return through Columbia from Mexico with gold and silver — in fact these expeditions included such Columbians as Young E. Hicks, Richard Gentry, and Samuel C. Lamme. The California Gold Rush swept with it a number of local residents, including William Garth, David Guitar, and Samuel Maupin. Businessman David Hickman operated a ferry across the North Platte River during the gold frenzy and during the 1850s hauled supplies for the army in western territories.

Excellent access to river routes also strengthened local trade. Goods shipped up the Missouri River landed at Providence in southern Boone County, and merchants like James L. Stephens, Sr., operated freight wagons to transport these supplies to Columbia. Moses Barth of Rocheport and other area retailers made frequent buying trips to Philadelphia via the river network. And the local farm economy shipped large quantities of tobacco, pork, wheat, whiskey, and other products downstream to New Orleans.

Despite the building of a plank road from Columbia to Providence and thus a better link to the river, in the 1850s Columbians lost their key location astride commercial routes. The company that constructed the first telegraph line west of St. Louis placed Jefferson City but not Columbia on its route in 1850, mainly because Columbians failed to purchase the firm's stock. That the railroads bypassed Columbia was more critical. As early as 1837 local enthusiasts including John B. Gordon, James S. Rollins, William F. Switzler, and Odon Guitar obtained legislative approval of a railroad to connect Columbia with Louisiana, Missouri, on the Mississippi River. That line and others never materialized, and the roads actually built across Missouri between 1851-1865 missed the city. A $200,000 inducement raised by city and county investors finally brought a branch of the North Missouri Railroad (later the Wabash) from Centralia to Columbia in 1867. Thirty-two years later a $20,000 "bonus" helped finance a branch of the Missouri, Kansas & Texas Railroad from McBaine to Columbia.

Thus Columbia never enjoyed mainline rail service. As long as trains carried the bulk of America's goods and passengers, from the 1860s to the 1920s, Columbia was "isolated in a railroad sense," as a 1908 statement phrased it. Such isolation meant that the city did not attract the factories of large corporations or the immigrants who might have worked in them. Essentially without industry, the city retained its character as a quiet residential community founded upon education.

A mixture of government, education, and private enterprise helped Columbia to benefit from 20th century revolutions in transportation and communications. In 1925 both Stephens and Christian colleges initiated radio programming (Stephens on its own station, KFRU), and in the 1950s the university initiated local television programming. The decisions of state and federal highway planners, whom Columbia leaders lobbied, also favored the city. In 1922 U.S. highways 40 and 63 intersected Columbia in the new national road network, and in the 1950s Interstate 70 passed through the city and commercial air service became available. Columbia has regained the transportation advantages which it lost with the coming of the railroads.

Transportation as well as agricultural processing facilities have helped Columbia function as the economic center of a rich agricultural region. From an early date farmers shipped crops and livestock through the city to distant markets. Also, before the Civil War farmers used the services of area tanneries, a hog processing plant, and a distillery located in the Rockbridge area south of town. Over the years an assortment of sawmills, flour mills, blacksmiths, and feed and seed dealers have served area farmers. The rural trade was important to downtown retailers as well. Merchants recognized the impact of farmer spending by helping to make

Opposite page, top: For years Columbia recognized the importance of agriculture to its economy by joining the university in sponsoring an annual Farmers Week, which featured speakers, entertainment, and information. A banner hangs over Broadway, looking east from near Eighth Street about 1913. From the A.M. Finley Photograph Albums, volume I. Courtesy, Joint Collection University of Missouri, Western Historical Manuscript Collection-Columbia, State Historical Society of Missouri Manuscripts

Opposite page, center: Television came to Columbia and central Missouri on December 21, 1953, when the university's station KOMU went on the air. The curators, led by broadcaster Lester E. Cox of Springfield, determined the direction of this laboratory for journalism students when they obtained network affiliation rather than educational status for the station. This view shows Dr. Edward C. Lambert, assistant to the president in charge of television, and a student. Courtesy, University of Missouri Archives

Opposite page, bottom: The Star Barber Shop, Henninger Jewelers, and The Drug Shop were among the business neighbors of Barths circa 1915. (Seventy years later Barths remains, while the others disappeared long ago.) Note the American flag—hanging behind what was probably a Fourth of July parade—which displays 48 stars. SHSM

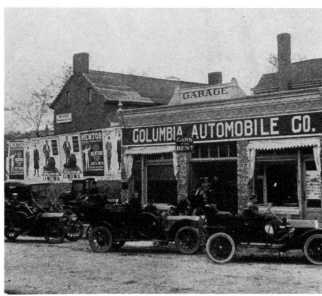

Above: Although it enjoyed less-than-ideal railway service, Columbia benefited from automobiles and hard-surfaced highways. Early car enthusiasts included blacksmith W.B. West, whose 1905 Oldsmobile was Columbia's first car, and John Allton, who also was a pioneer airplane pilot. Frederick W. Neidermeyer—lawyer, Columbia mayor, and president of the school board—owned the city's first car dealership, the Columbia Automobile Company on South Ninth Street, pictured here circa 1910. From Columbia: The Coming City of Central Missouri, 1910. Courtesy, Carol Crabb

William Hirth appears in this detail of a portrait painted by Columbia artist Sidney Larson and owned by the Missouri Farmers' Associaton. A national figure in farm politics, Hirth advocated the idea of federal governmental action to raise farm prices. Hirth bitterly rejected Republican farm policy during the 1920s and championed Franklin Roosevelt in 1932, although he became disillusioned with the New Deal during the 1930s. SHSM

county fair week a tribute to agricultural productivity. The town and the countryside developed a mutually beneficial interdependence.

Columbia's importance as an agribusiness center is perhaps best symbolized by the founding and early growth of the Missouri Farmers' Association (MFA). William A. Hirth, who moved to Columbia shortly after the turn of the century and briefly practiced law, turned to newspaper publishing. Believing that he understood the causes of low farm income, Hirth preached a gospel of organization and cooperation among the state's farmers through his newspaper, *The Missouri Farmer*. By buying and selling through "clubs," Hirth believed, farmers could overcome their impotence as single purchasers (of seed) and marketers (of wheat and corn). Hirth organized the first Farm Club in 1914 in Chariton County. Missouri farmers responded quickly: by September 1920, 34,242 of them belonged to the Missouri Farmers' Association, the statewide organization formed in 1917 to unite the local clubs. Until his death in 1940, Hirth directed the co-ops of the MFA from his Columbia office, and became a national figure in the turbulent farm politics of the 1920s and 1930s.

The Kentuckians who settled Columbia and Boone County brought with them an interest in developing purebred livestock and in agricultural improvement generally. Not only was horse racing early Columbians' most popular form of entertainment, but these interests led, in 1835, to the formation of the Boone County Agricultural Society and, on October 16 and 17, Missouri's first county fair. Held originally on the racetrack grounds in southeast Columbia, the annual exhibition of farm products has continued—with interruptions and changes of location—to the present day. During the 1870s and 1880s black farmers, organized in the Boone County Colored Agricultural and Mechanical Association, held their own fairs in Columbia.

Although the business interests of some Columbia merchants reached beyond the city, most retailers served a local clientele. By the 1830s and 1840s consumers could do business with a dozen general merchandise stores and an assortment of specialty shops that were clustered on Broadway. In 1901 Columbia retailers operated two music stores, two department stores, three meat markets, 17 grocery stores, three hardware outlets, three shoe stores, three lumberyards, two bookstores, and three saloons, among others. Although whites owned most retail establishments, after 1865 black-owned businesses north of Broadway and west of Eighth Street served Columbia's black neighborhood. In 1917, for example, blacks owned several barber shops, a beauty parlor, a pool hall, three cafes, a laundry, a carpentry shop, a drug store, a grocery, and three dray services (which met incoming trains). Dr. J.A. Taylor operated a medical practice on South Eighth Street. Also, many Columbia businesses depended upon the student trade, especially as the number of students and their discretionary spending increased in the 20th century. "In Columbia we have approximately a 60 percent interest by the retailer in University students," a clothing store manager estimated in 1932.

Columbia's retail businesses have undergone continual turnover. One observer wrote in 1895: "Of the establishments that were here 25 years ago only three remain. Nearly all the business portion has been burned and rebuilt. . . ." But some retail businesses have survived. Three, the present Neates and Barths clothing stores and Buchroeders Jewelers, are among the survivors that originated in the 19th century. One man who built a long-lasting retail outlet and the structure which it occupied at Eighth and Broadway was Charles B. Miller of the Miller Shoe Company. Typical of several generations of downtown merchants as civic leaders, Miller served on the Columbia Board of Education, helped to form the Retail Merchants Association, and belonged to the Round Table Club, the Elks, the Columbia Country Club, the Commercial Club, and the Rotary Club. Miller served as a director of the Boone County National Bank and as a Deacon in the Presbyterian Church. Downtown Columbia is a monument to people like Charles Miller.

Columbia's service-based economy includes strong banking, insurance, and medical-care sectors, all of which began their growth in the 19th century. During the city's early decades most citizens had no need of banking services, and those who wished to borrow money obtained loans from wealthy merchants. When banks did appear in Columbia—Moss Prewitt and his sons-in-law James H. Parker and Robert B. Price operated the first one beginning in 1856—they served mostly affluent families. Not until early in the 20th century did such institutions as the Boone County National Bank, the Central Bank, and the Exchange National Bank extend checking accounts and loans to the average family. Insurance, another of Columbia's service industries, also began in the 1850s. The threat of loss from fire prompted local citizens to organize the Boone County Home Mutual Fire Insurance Company in 1851. Columbians founded several other local fire insurance companies and became agents for large national firms after the Civil War, a period when insurance policies began to protect against hazards other than fire.

Although Columbians enjoyed competent medical care from an early date, the city was without a hospital until the 20th century. Pioneer medical practitioners included the versatile Dr. William Jewell, who moved to Columbia in 1822, and Drs. William H. Duncan and James H. Bennett, both trained at the University of Pennsylvania. A dentist, Dr. S.W. Comfort, conducted a practice during the 1830s. Columbia's reputation as a regional medical center grew with increasing numbers of practitioners and the university's acquisition of a medical school in 1873. Columbia in 1909, with a population of less than 10,000, supported 30 physicians and surgeons and six dentists.

The University of Missouri built Columbia's first hospital, Parker Memorial Hospital, with a $15,000 gift from local resident William H. Parker in 1901. Primarily a teaching facility that treated charity cases and referral

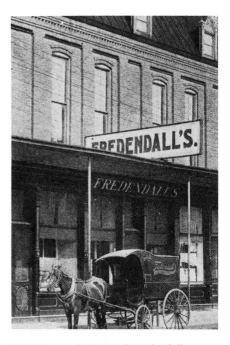

Abraham and Winifred Fredendall operated a retail department store, first on South Ninth Street, pictured here, and later on Broadway. Fredendalls offered consumers a variety of merchandise under one roof, free delivery by a one-horse-power conveyance, and a covered sidewalk. Late 20th century shoppers still enjoy the first and third of these features in the city's retail areas. From Picturesque Columbia: Souvenir Gems of 1900, SHSM

Right: Another durable retail business is the Neates store on Broadway, which has operated since the 1860s. Mr. S. Frank Neate, leaning on the counter at the left in this circa 1910 photograph, first worked for the Strawn-Holland Dry Goods Company and eventually bought the business. His son Sidney B. Neate continues in business at the same location in the 1980s. Courtesy, Sidney B. Neate

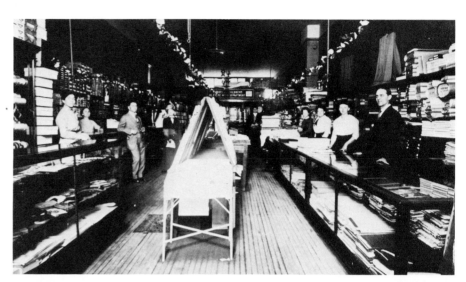

Above: This musician advertised the Boone County Fair from the back of a truck in 1948. By that time the fair had moved to its present site on Clinkscales Road. With the promotional help of such people as Robert E. Lee Hill, the fair became the occasion for celebrating one of the county's unique culinary delights, the Boone County Ham. Courtesy, Stephens College Archives

Below: The construction of the university's Brewer Field House in 1929 provided area merchants with a large indoor display area for auto and home shows, like the one pictured in the mid-1930s. These shows, which continue decades later, illustrate Columbia's tradition of town-gown cooperation. Courtesy, Columbia Chamber of Commerce

patients from throughout the state, Parker Hospital served Columbians adequately until the World War I era. A 1917 state law that encouraged the establishment of county hospitals, along with the disastrous flu epidemic of 1918, prompted Boone Countians to construct a medical facility of their own. Bond issues approved by county voters in 1919 and 1920 financed the Boone County Hospital. The 65-bed unit opened in December 1921. Its board of trustees, which included Columbians Hartley H. Banks and North Todd Gentry, set the daily room rate at $2.50. When Dr. and Mrs. Frank G. Nifong gave the hospital $100,000 for construction of a new wing in 1954, they reaffirmed the continuing support that Columbians have given to the county medical complex.

Local support brought a state medical facility to town in 1939. Beginning in 1937 the Columbia Chamber of Commerce—the onetime Commercial Club—began working to locate a proposed state cancer hospital in Columbia. Chamber members identified several potential sites, convinced officials from Jefferson City to locate the facility on property facing Highway 40, and persuaded the city government to purchase the land and donate it to the hospital commission. The Ellis Fischel State Cancer Hospital opened in 1940. As had occurred before, joint private and public effort resulted in a new facility for the city.

Two of Columbia's most important industries have been construction and publishing. For decades colleges have guaranteed Columbia an uncommonly large number of major construction projects, and a growing city required new housing for its citizens. In early 1910 a local writer grew lyrical over the approaching construction season: "In a few more weeks the sound of thousands of hammers will fill the air and the song of the hod carrier will be heard upon every hand." It is not known if hod carriers sang at their work, but a succession of courthouses, theaters, classroom buildings, dormitories, and hotels provided steady employment for such workers and profits for their employers. Columbia's several newspapers made the city a minor publishing center by the 1880s, but the E.W. Stephens Publishing Company made it an important one. The firm printed legislative debates and court records from states as far away as Oregon, as well as a myriad of other publications. In 1921 the company was the city's third largest employer, with 125 people on its payroll. In that year 182 of Columbia's 810 hourly wage earners worked in publishing.

For over a century Columbia's leaders have worked to bring industry to the city. In 1869 a public meeting considered establishing an Immigration Society to attract workers to Columbia. In 1873 the city government, believing that Columbia "should give every possible encouragement toward fostering a spirit of manufacturing industries," offered tax advantages to new industry. But until after World War II such efforts, with one exception, came to little. The exception was the establishment of the Hamilton-Brown Shoe Company factory in 1906-1907. Officials of this St. Louis firm, at the time the world's largest manufacturer of shoes,

Left: From 1910 to 1955, medical students could obtain only the two pre-clinical years of instruction at the university in Columbia. With the completion of the medical center in 1956, a complete course of study was introduced, and the city began to benefit from its new status as a major supplier of quality medical care. Courtesy, Social Sciences-History Department, Stephens College

Below far left: The careers open to young women during the 1920s varied according to the women's education and race. While blacks performed domestic chores in homes or at the colleges, whites filled positions as clerks in stores or operatives in the shoe factory. Pictured is an office worker of the late 1920s using a dictaphone. Courtesy, Stephens College Archives

Below left: Both men and women found work at the new Hamilton-Brown shoe factory, although only men appear in this photo of the lasting department. The company competed with local banks by offering workers a savings plan that paid six percent interest on all deposits (in 1910!). From The H-B Idea, 1910, SHSM

notified the Commercial Club in the summer of 1906 that it wished to build a branch factory in a Missouri or Illinois town. The community selected would raise $60,000 to build the plant, provide a railroad siding, and supply low-cost utilities and workers. The club spearheaded an intense and successful drive to raise the money in September and October, and workers erected the factory building at Wilkes Boulevard and Fay Street during the winter. Optimistic Columbians envisioned a new era for the city. The shoe factory would help diversify the economy, stimulate growth for the entire community, and provide employment for young Columbians not bound for college. Although it did these things, Hamilton-Brown did not chart new directions for the city's economy. The company was Columbia's only monument to assembly-line mass production at the time; it rarely employed more than half the number of workers that it had promised; and it closed during the Great Depression—temporarily in 1931, permanently in 1939. But for the factory's closing, Columbia withstood the Depression without permanent damage to large employers.

Columbia's labor force, given the importance of education, retailing, and medical care, has been predominantly professional and white-collar. In 1921, for example, the university alone employed approximately 350 administrators, faculty, and office personnel, compared with Hamilton-Brown's 340 operatives and supervisors. Secretaries, retail clerks, nurses, and teachers have been more representative of Columbia's workers than blue-collar laborers. Labor unions in the building and printing trades have a long and successful history in Columbia. In 1917, for example, all of Columbia's labor organizations were in these trades with the exception of the barbers' union.

From an economy which initially relied upon agriculture and mercantile pursuits, Columbia has diversified over a period of 160 years. Construction, insurance, medical care, and publishing remain important categories of employment and enterprise in the late 20th century, but the strength of each depends in some measure upon the existence and vitality of Columbia's major endeavor, education. The story of education in Columbia deserves special treatment.

CHAPTER FOUR
The Schools and Colleges

In the 19th century, student life in the colleges centered around the intellectual and social activities of literary societies. Six students and Professor Joseph K. Rogers founded the Martha Washington Society at Christian College in 1857. The society's members were photographed on February 22, 1889; George Washington's birthday was also the date of the group's most important annual "open meeting," which university men were welcome to attend. Courtesy, Office of Public Relations, Columbia College

Since the mid-19th century, educational institutions have fueled Columbia's economic growth, shaped its social and cultural life, determined its residential patterns, and provided its recreation. However, Columbia was not merely the fortunate-but-passive recipient of institutions planted here by the Missouri General Assembly and religious groups. The reality behind such slogans as "the Athens of Missouri" and "Collegetown, U.S.A." is that the schools and colleges that Columbia's early settlers created are truly Boone County's and Columbia's own.

An interest in education is as old as the town. The original plan of 1821 shows 10 acres optimistically reserved as the site of a state university, and during the 1820s affluent families patronized several private academies. To some Columbians, education had a loftier purpose than career preparation. Education was toasted on July 4, 1831, as follows: "As knowledge is justly conceived to be the basis of public happiness, the promotion of science and literature is consequently the surest guarantee of a free, efficient, and equal government." Schools established in the early 1830s embodied this belief and laid the foundations of Columbia's schools and colleges.

Out of a mass meeting held in August 1831 came the idea to found a young men's academy. While citizens subscribed funds, campaign leaders obtained a legislative charter and erected a brick building. Columbia College began its first term in November 1834 under the presidency of Thomas Miller, recently of Kentucky's Transylvania University. By then Columbia had a school for young women, the Columbian Female Academy—established at another public meeting in August 1833—which opened that autumn under the direction of Principal Lucy Ann Wales. Meeting originally in the Presbyterian church, the school occupied its own building (today part of the Niedermeyer Apartments) at Tenth and Cherry from 1837 to 1855. Finally, Columbia's common or public school held its first session in the Columbia College building between January 20 and April 11, 1834. In about 1836 the school overseers constructed a two-room building at Second and Broadway, which was until 1871 Columbia's only public schoolhouse.

During the 1830s Missouri legislators fought over the location and financing of a state university. Boone County, with its central location, a large and prosperous population, and an already functioning college that could become the university's nucleus, was attractive as a potential site. During his first term in the lower house of the General Assembly, Columbia's James S. Rollins in 1839 helped to formulate the procedure

Below: The university's annual enrollment during the 1840s averaged 90 students. In the war year of 1862, four faculty members taught 50 students. Periods of rapid growth included the early 20th century, when enrollment topped and then greatly exceeded 1,000, and the post-World War II years, when the basement of Crowder Hall became a temporary cafeteria, pictured. In 1946-1947, 7,000 of the 11,000 university students had served during the war. Courtesy, University of Missouri Archives

Above: This W.J. Hennessy drawing of a country school, which appeared in Every Saturday magazine in 1871, depicts the primitive facilities of Columbia's first public school. For years the school did not provide a truly universal, completely tax-supported education: not everyone could afford the $2.50-per-term tuition in 1834, for example. Many young people continued to receive instruction at home and training as apprentices. SHSM

used to locate the proposed institution. The law authorized six central Missouri counties to bid for the university by raising cash and other assets sufficient to establish a state university. Boone County residents pledged cash, land, and buildings; only 19 promised amounts of over $1,000 apiece. When the state commissioners received the bids in June, Boone County's was the largest, at $118,300. The successful campaign became a source of enduring pride for local residents. Local citizens honored nearly all of the substantial pledge, money which the legislature was unable to raise and which gave Missouri a university—the first state university established west of the Mississippi River. On July 4, 1843, a parade wound from the courthouse through the small town to the new campus on the south side, where visitors joined Columbians to dedicate the main building.

Columbia's direct support of the university continued long after payment of the initial subscription. Not until 1867 did the legislature make its first appropriation for the school, eloquent expression of a statewide feeling that it was not Missouri's, but Boone County's, university. The county accepted the responsibility. "Time and again," a writer recalled in 1910, "the hat was passed among the citizens of Columbia to help pay the salaries of professors." On two occasions in particular, local campaigns first enlarged and then saved the university. Local residents raised $89,500 to locate the College of Agriculture in Columbia in 1870, and they raised $50,000 to help the state rebuild the university after the disasterous fire of 1892. Columbia dollars thus built or helped build Switzler Hall and Jesse Hall. In both 1870 and 1892 the willingness of local residents to support the university, together with Boone County's able representation in Jefferson City, defeated attempts to locate part or all of the institution in another city.

Since both Columbia College and the University of Missouri (until 1868) excluded female students, families who wished to educate daughters established institutions geared to women's education. This motive and the rivalry among Columbia's Protestants produced Christian Female College and the Columbia Baptist Female College in the 1850s.

In 1849 leaders of the Disciples of Christ (Christian) church gained control of a community movement to provide college instruction for young women. Christian Female College opened on April 7, 1851, in the Christian church building. Later that year the college acquired the unfinished residence and grounds of Dr. James H. Bennett as its campus, the location which the present Columbia College occupies. Christian College was the first women's college to be chartered by a state legislature west of the Mississippi River. After the Columbia Female Academy closed in 1855, the school's Baptist and other denominational supporters felt the need of a female college with a religious orientation different from Christian's. In the fall of 1856 they opened the Baptist Female College in the old Academy building, which they left for the former home of Oliver Parker in 1857. The Stephens College South Campus still occupies the former Parker property.

Like the university, the two female colleges depended upon local support. While both institutions long enjoyed close ties with strong Missouri denominations, they received little financial support from the Christians and Baptists. Only the leadership and generosity of local congregations and individuals allowed the women's colleges to survive almost constant economic hardship during their early decades. The Baptist College became Stephens College in 1870 when James L. Stephens, Sr., provided an endowment.

Who were the Columbia and county residents who had founded four private schools, the state university, and the district common school by 1856? Those who led the public campaigns were all male, although they enjoyed the support of wives and daughters and employed women teachers in the female and public schools. For most of them, founding schools was of a piece with building railroads and other activities which promoted the community's development. With a few exceptions they were not professional educators, but rather farmers, merchants, lawyers, and clergymen. Over a period of 150 years many Columbia and county residents, both male and female, have served as trustees, curators, donors, alumni(ae) leaders of local schools, and parents to new generations of students.

The political and social disorder which accompanied the Civil War in Boone County took its toll on education. Most seriously affected of Columbia's institutions was the district school. Ironically, the generous support which Columbians gave to academies and colleges undermined the public school. Choosing private education for their children, the town's leading families lacked enthusiasm for educating the children of others at public expense. School trustees even closed the building at Second and Broadway from 1856 to 1859, when the university's primary department admitted Columbia's students in return for the district's share of state school funds. Two years after the district school resumed classes the war erupted, and from 1861 to 1867 there was no public primary school in Columbia.

The University of Missouri closed its doors from March to November 1862, as federal troops camped on the grounds and used the president's house as their headquarters and Academic Hall as a storehouse and military prison. Although the Christian and Baptist colleges remained open, they suffered reduced enrollments and income. Teachers who had no guarantee of salary payments remained at their posts, helping students tend gardens which provided food for the college. All three institutions suffered from real or imagined ties to the Confederacy. It did not help the university's image in some parts of Missouri that students demonstrated in favor of the Southern cause in the spring of 1861, that two Boone County curators— Eli Bass and Walter T. Lenoir—resigned after failing to pledge their loyalty

Right: On the evening of Saturday, January 9, 1892, a fire that began in the electric wiring in the chapel's ceiling destroyed Academic Hall. Pictured are the remains of Academic Hall on January 10. A letter dated January 11 assured students' parents that university officials and "the generosity of the citizens of Columbia" had provided classroom space in churches, the courthouse, and other buildings. Demolition crews left the 1842 columns, which still serve as a Columbia landmark today. SHSM

Far right: Until the 1930s the university provided few dormitory buildings, and not until after World War II did Columbia have many apartments. Thus, for years students lived in boarding houses and roomed with private families, especially on the south side of town. This diligent engineering student rented a room at 1205 Paquin Street in 1905. SHSM

Left: The colleges' traditions also became the town's, and no season of the year was filled with more time-honored rituals than the annual spring commencement. The photo shows the cutting of the Ivy Chain at Christian College in the late 1920s or early 1930s. The custom, begun in 1900, symbolized the separation of each graduate from her classmates and her entry into the larger world beyond the campus. Courtesy, Office of Public Relations, Columbia College

Left: Although Columbia has long been noted for its achievements in the higher education of women, female students have had to endure the belittling attitudes suggested by this circa 1920 parade float. These university students were participating in the annual Farmers' Fair, a regular feature of the College of Agriculture's calendar from 1905 to 1958. SHSM, gift of Robert L. Price

Below left: From their earliest days the women's colleges took the education of women seriously. A male who attended Christian's first public final examinations in 1852 marveled that the "young ladies. . .are compelled to think." Both schools explored nontraditional vocations for women. Stephens offered flight training, initially as a wartime program, from 1943 to 1961. Courtesy, Stephens College Archives

to the Union, and that Confederate sympathizers were numerous in the university's host community. Legislators who later opposed locating the College of Agriculture in Columbia had excellent recall of such incidents. Although they maintained a careful neutrality, the women's colleges also suffered reprisals. Following the Confederate raid on the courthouse in 1862, Colonel Lewis Merrill threatened to close Christian College. Robert L. Todd, Mrs. Abraham Lincoln's first cousin, allegedly obtained a letter from the Commander-in-Chief forbidding such action. Merrill did close the Baptist College for three days after two of its local students shouted a rebel yell at passing troops.

Just as education was a high priority for Columbia's earliest white settlers, blacks also established schools at the first opportunity. Although the former slaves received support and encouragement from some whites, black efforts produced black schools. Education was an early subject of community meetings in 1865, within months of the war's end, and both Methodists and Baptists sponsored classes during the following year. It was the Baptist school, organized in the home of John Lang, Sr., and supported by tax revenue as early as 1867, which emerged as Columbia's black school. Known first as the Cummings Academy—named for Charles E. Cummings, its principal from 1867 to 1876—the institution later became the Excelsior School and, in 1898, the Frederick Douglass School. From Lang's house, classes moved to a building constructed at Third and Ash in 1868 with money raised by blacks locally and a grant arranged by William F. Switzler from the Freedmen's Bureau in Washington. In 1885 the school relocated in a new structure built by the school district at Third and Park Avenue. Although it added a high school curriculum to its primary course by the end of the century, the Douglass School suffered from inadequate facilities and discriminatory teacher salaries, among other things. But achievements were real. Literacy rates among young people far exceeded those of their parents late in the 19th century, for example, and Douglass was one of the few black high school programs in outstate Missouri in 1900.

School segregation, while required by the state, also reaffirmed Columbia's southern roots. But the community shared little with the Deep South, where violent resistance often met court-ordered integration. As early as the 1940s the Columbia schools began easing the dual-educational system, as black and white teachers met together on curricular matters and students of both races joined in some extra-curricular activities. Local school officials quickly endorsed, though only gradually implemented, the May 1954 Supreme Court decision outlawing segregated public education. In July the school board adopted a *laissez faire* approach to integration: black parents would determine the location and speed of the process as they transferred their children from Douglass to previously all-white schools. In time the excessive cost of low-enrollment programs at Douglass would force their elimination. In 1960 and 1962, respectively, the board

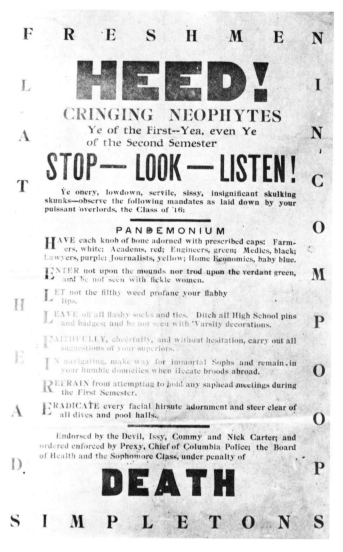

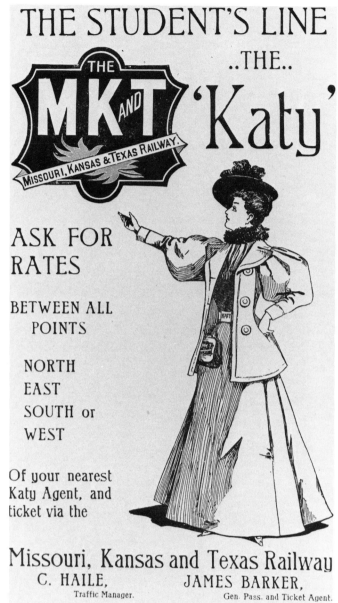

University social life had become highly structured and ritualized by the eve of World War I. The hazing of freshman students was one tradition that has since disappeared. This warning poster greeted members of the class of 1917 when they enrolled in the fall of 1913. From the A.M. Finley Photograph Albums, volume I. Courtesy, Joint Collection University of Missouri, Western Historical Manuscript Collection-Columbia, State Historical Society of Missouri Manuscripts

Some 19th century Missourians argued that Columbia was too isolated a location for the university—an argument which had some merit, although it often hid other dissatisfactions and jealousies. But out-of-state students found their way to Columbia as early as the 1840s, and by the turn of the century two railroads competed for student business. The Katy published this advertisement in 1900. Courtesy, Stephens College Archives

James Leechman Stephens, Sr.—merchant, real estate developer, and Baptist lay leader—began a long family association with the college that bore his name. Son Edwin W. and grandson Hugh served as presidents of the board of curators from 1917 to 1947. SHSM

A group of triumphant sophomores has mail-boxed a freshman across Conley Avenue from Jesse Hall in 1913. One can only guess the reaction of university president A. Ross Hill, had he glanced at the scene through his office window. From the A.M. Finley Photograph Albums, volume I. Courtesy, Joint Collection University of Missouri, Western Historical Manuscript Collection-Columbia, State Historical Society of Missouri Manuscripts

Above: The first grade class of the Jefferson Elementary School posed beside the building in 1910 for this photo. The girl marked with an "X" in the second row was Mary Brady, who as Mary Brady Biggs served as the first elementary art coordinator in the Columbia schools from 1937 to 1969. Courtesy, Mary Brady Biggs

Above left: This is the 1885 Frederick Douglass school building as it appeared on March 12, 1908. Located at Third Street (Providence Road) and Park Avenue, Douglass stood near Flat Branch Creek, visible in the foreground. In 1916 the first portion of the present Douglass building replaced this structure. Frederick Douglass escaped slavery in Maryland and became an articulate abolitionist and civil rights leader, one who served as a model for blacks in central Missouri and throughout the nation. Courtesy, Horticulture Department, University of Missouri-Columbia and State Historical Society of Missouri

More than twice as many students enrolled in the district's schools in 1912 as had done so in 1895. A new elementary school to serve the Stewart and other west-side subdivisions (and named for Ulysses S. Grant to balance the Robert E. Lee school on the east side) opened in 1910. This is Grant's fifth-grade class celebrating Halloween in about 1913. Courtesy, Mary Brady Biggs

Above: Anna Forney, a Stephens College student from Arkansas, used this ticket to attend the Missouri-Kansas football game in 1915. After attending the contest she recorded the afternoon's losses: "Kansas won in terrible storm. Expense: Ticket $2.00; Hat (ruined) 5.00; Gloves (ruined) 1.00; Suit Pressed .50" From the scrapbook of Anna Forney. Courtesy, Stephens College Archives

closed the Douglass high school and junior high school. And 13 years after the court decision of 1954, partially in response to public pressure, officials phased out the elementary classes. Throughout these years the board reassigned Douglass's teachers to other schools and involved black and white parents in the integration process. Although blacks lost an important community institution when Douglass closed, integration gave tangible meaning to the ideal of equality taught in Columbia's classrooms and the dream of opportunity celebrated by business groups.

The white schools attracted greater numbers of students and public support after the Civil War. The community's increasing willingness to spend money was an important development. In the late 1860s, shabby and scattered classroom facilities epitomized the discouraging state of Columbia's public schools. Three primary schools served white students, including the old and crowded 1836 building and the basement of the Methodist church at Sixth and Broadway. The church functioned as the city's largest school for a decade after voters approved its purchase in 1871. In 1872 and 1873 Columbians, acting under a recent state law, organized a school district and elected a school board. Voters began authorizing the construction of new classroom buildings in 1881 — the first in 45 years — when the district purchased land at Eighth and Rogers streets and erected Jefferson Elementary School. Between 1896 and 1935 the school district constructed 11 other classroom buildings. These included the city's first high school, built in 1899 to offer coursework no longer available at the university, and David H. Hickman High School, which opened in 1927. During these years Columbians committed themselves to a quality educational program conducted in excellent facilities.

Columbia's women's colleges also grew larger and stronger following the Civil War. Both found able and determined presidents in times of financial stress and curricular change. James Madison Wood led Stephens from 1912 to 1947, during which time enrollment grew from a handful to well over 1,000 and the campus expanded to the northeast of the original property. At Christian, Luella St. Clair succeeded her late husband as president in 1893. During her three separate presidential terms, which ended in 1920, she raised the money to erect the eight buildings which housed the college for more than a half-century. By the 1940s Christian's enrollment averaged about 350 students annually.

In numerous ways Columbians sustained the growth of these colleges. Money raised locally, for example, helped to build their attractive campuses, support which Stephens recognized in 1920 by naming a new dormitory "Columbia Hall." In turn, increasing college enrollments spurred the city's economic growth. Merchants estimated in the early 1920s that students spent over $2 million annually in Columbia. Student spending power occasionally had unexpected consequences. In the late 1930s some Stephens students roomed at the Daniel Boone Tavern. Management changed the business's name to the Daniel Boone "Hotel"

Right: The presence of the colleges has shaped many Columbia businesses. Frank Balsamo, Sr., a native of Sicily who came to Columbia in 1918, owned the University Fruit Company in 1921. A retail outlet located at 921 East Broadway from 1919 to 1956, the firm evolved into a wholesale supplier to student dining facilities in dormitories, fraternities, and sororities. Courtesy, Lud Balsamo, Frank Balsamo, Jr., and Larry Balsamo

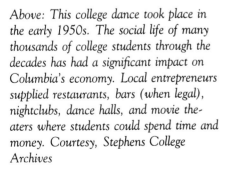

Above: This college dance took place in the early 1950s. The social life of many thousands of college students through the decades has had a significant impact on Columbia's economy. Local entrepreneurs supplied restaurants, bars (when legal), nightclubs, dance halls, and movie theaters where students could spend time and money. Courtesy, Stephens College Archives

Right: Walter Williams left the School of Journalism in 1930 to become the university's president. As a resident of Columbia for 40 years, he was an effective liaison with the local community. In this circa 1930 view Williams, seated second from the right, and Sarah Lockwood Williams entertain several local business and professional men at their home on South Glenwood Avenue. SHSM

Left: As this photo of a radio workshop at Christian College in 1950 suggests, Columbia's colleges have offered unique programs to their undergraduates. For decades Christian and Stephens taught equestrian science, while the university enrolled both men and women in military science programs in the late 19th century. Christian offered a pioneer class in journalism before the university had a journalism school. Courtesy, Office of Public Relations, Columbia College

Above: American educators introduced methods of "learning by doing" after the turn of the century, and in Columbia a leading innovator was Ella Victoria Dobbs. Her work in the elementary schools from 1910 to 1913 still bore fruit in 1946 when these second-grade children at Field School ran a store. Dobbs was a university professor of industrial art, a local women's suffrage leader, and in 1920 the first woman to run for the school board. Courtesy, Mary Brady Biggs

Above: The family of Dr. Stanley Smith (pictured), Columbia's mayor from 1905 to 1907 and from 1909 to 1911, illustrates the variety of town-gown ties. Smith's father, Fielding Smith, was a Stephens curator. After retiring from his practice, Dr. Smith taught in the School of Veterinary Medicine. Mrs. Smith was president of the Christian College Club. And Queen Smith, a Christian graduate and the Smiths' daughter, taught in the Journalism School. A complex web of relationships has united Columbia and its colleges. Courtesy, Queen Smith

Opposite page: Nowadays, springtime commencements call forth light, often colorful clothing that disappears under black academic robes during graduation ceremonies. Christian College's graduating seniors of 1889 had no need of hot and heavy robes, however, as basic black was the fashionable norm. College President William A. Oldham poses with the class. Courtesy, Office of Public Relations, Columbia College

when parents objected to their daughters' letters bearing a saloon's letterhead.

The Great Depression of the 1930s proved that if the colleges' growth benefited the city, retrenchment hurt it. Not since the Civil War had an external crisis so seriously threatened Columbia's educational institutions, and although even the private colleges survived, they did so at a cost. Both the university and the public school system experienced reduced state and local tax revenues. During 1931 Governor Henry S. Caulfield cut $900,000 from the university's 1931-1932 biennial appropriation of $3.3 million. Administrators at all the schools made personnel reductions, and remaining staff coped with smaller salaries and wages. Both the public schools and the university, believing men to be family breadwinners, adopted policies which under certain conditions denied female employees their jobs.

The University of Missouri became a true university in the post-Civil War decades with the addition of professional colleges to the original liberal arts curriculum. Columbia has had special relationships with several of these schools. The College of Normal Instruction (founded in 1867) supplied Columbia's schools with teachers and expertise in establishing and evaluating programs. The College of Agriculture (1870) trained Boone County farmers in modern farming techniques and helped make Columbia the state's agricultural center. The College of Medicine (1873) supplied Columbia with trained personnel and gave the town its first hospital.

Columbia professionals helped establish several of the university's schools. Lawyer Boyle Gordon joined the Law School's first faculty. Nathaniel Patten's *Missouri Intelligencer* (1830), William F. Switzler's *Missouri Statesman* (1842), Edwin W. Stephens' *Columbia Missouri Herald* (1871), and Edwin M. Watson's *Columbia Daily Tribune* (1901) were regionally important newspapers that created an environment of journalistic excellence. Both Stephens and Walter Williams, the *Herald*'s editor, beginning in 1889, were university curators and officials of the Missouri Press Association, a longtime advocate of professional training for journalists. Their leadership helped to establish the world's first degree-granting school of journalism at the university in 1908. Dr. Andrew W. McAlester initiated plans for a medical school in 1872 at a meeting of Boone County's Medical Society, and Dr. Thomas A. Arnold joined McAlester on the first medical faculty. In the same year Williams, the school's first dean, founded the *Columbia Missourian*.

That the earliest southern migrants to a primitive western frontier cared deeply about education is a useful fact for later generations, challenged by high educational costs, to remember. But equally important is the truth that Columbians themselves brought their educational institutions into being and, at some critical junctures, were instrumental in their survival and expansion. Missouri has the first state university founded west of the

Mississippi River, the first journalism school in the world, and other educational distinctions—and for these it can thank Boone County and Columbia. That the city has been a center of women's education for one-and-a-half centuries reflects credit on local patrons of the Columbia Female Academy, Stephens College, and Christian College. In 1921 a group portraying Columbia to outsiders stated: "Education is the corner-stone upon which the community has been built." To be fully accurate, this claim should have asserted that local citizens actively shaped and laid that cornerstone.

CHAPTER FIVE

The Spiritual and Cultural Life

Both women's colleges, wishing to offer their students what the coeducational university did not, developed strong conservatories of music beginning in the 1880s. Christian offered a three-year program in voice, stringed instruments, and pipe organ, as well as a concert series. This is the Stephens orchestra, perhaps the city's first, circa 1900. Courtesy, Stephens College Archives

Since its earliest days, Columbia, with a southern population predominantly Baptist, Christian (the Disciples of Christ), Methodist, and Presbyterian, has been an evangelical Protestant community. These denominations rejected elaborate church hierarchies and a formal liturgical style of worship in favor of congregational autonomy, scriptural fundamentalism, and the revival meeting. In later decades the city's religious life diversified, as other Christian denominations, Jews, and Muslims practiced their faiths. The migration of students and faculty, rather than an influx of European immigrants, created religious variety. But even with such changes, evangelical Protestantism remained the most prominent style of religious worship in Columbia.

Columbia's four pioneer congregations had organized by 1835. Led by Anderson Woods, Charles Hardin, and William Jewell, Baptists founded Columbia's first and the county's third church on November 22, 1823. As did the Methodists, Catholics, and other groups, Baptists worshiped in private homes and the courthouse until they could afford to erect a building. In 1836 Jewell and Moses U. Payne, a Methodist layman whose congregation had formed during the early 1830s, built Union Church on the south side of Walnut between Seventh and Eighth. Both groups worshiped there for about a decade. Columbia's Presbyterians organized the city's second congregation on September 14, 1828, when two missionaries from New York met with local laymen including Peter Wright and John and Elizabeth Sutton. In 1833 the Presbyterians built the city's first house of worship, a brick building located on the north side of Walnut between Fifth and Sixth. In 1834 the congregation held Boone County's first camp meeting three miles northeast of Columbia. Inspired by the visit of a Disciples of Christ minister in July 1831, local Disciples organized during 1832. In 1845 Alexander Campbell, a founder of the Disciples, spoke in Columbia.

Remarkably, 150 years after their founding, these four congregations still worship in central Columbia, a few blocks from their original meeting sites. The Baptists owned a church on the courthouse square from the 1850s until 1891, when they relocated at Broadway and Waugh Street. From 1846 until 1966, when they moved to Hitt Street, Presbyterians successively occupied two structures at 10th and Broadway. Since 1860 two different Christian church buildings have stood at 10th and Walnut. The Methodists occupied three locations on Broadway from about 1850 until 1930, when they moved to Ninth and Locust.

One of Boone County's first citizens, Anderson Woods, settled on Thrall's Prairie west of Columbia in 1816. Although he was a member of the first Boone County Court in 1820, Woods' primary work was religious. He was a founder of the three oldest congregations in the county—all Baptist—and the first pastor of one, the Columbia Baptist Church. Courtesy, Sidney B. Neate

Opposite page, bottom: Many Columbia and Boone County residents have retained an avid interest in outdoor skills and pastimes that were more than recreation to the earliest settlers. Game abounds for hunting, and streams like Perche, Hinkson, and Cedar Creeks have long served for fishing. These men fished for bass circa 1910. From Columbia: The Coming City of Central Missouri, 1910. Courtesy, Carol Crabb

Close ties between colleges and churches helped to keep these congregations centrally located. Near the Christian and Baptist churches were Christian and Stephens colleges. Several of Stephens' early presidents were concurrently pastors of the Baptist church, while early university presidents had close ties to leading Protestant denominations—like Samuel S. Laws, an ordained Presbyterian minister. The Calvary Episcopal Church moved from Broadway into a new building at Ninth and Locust in 1899 to be nearer the university, as did the Methodists three decades later. To serve better the town's temporary young residents, the Baptists built a student center in 1927, while Catholics erected a Knights of Columbus residence hall on College Avenue in 1920.

Columbians of other faiths formed congregations and built structures in the 19th and 20th centuries. Organized in May 1855, Calvary Episcopal acquired its first building in 1872. Catholics celebrated Mass in Columbia as early as 1835 and worshiped regularly beginning in 1876, opening the first Sacred Heart building in 1880. Lutherans did not form a congregation until 1925. Jews, who had held services in homes for years, met regularly in the YMCA building by 1926. The group consisted of about 50 townspeople and students. Congregations of the Church of God and the Seventh Day Adventists also appeared after 1880.

In this more diversified environment Columbia's oldest denominations grew larger, in part by adding new congregations. The Wilkes Boulevard Methodist church organized in 1910, following an open-air revival, and moved into its building in 1912. It served the northern section of the city whose shoe-factory workers lacked churches. A 1924 Columbia church survey found 13 white and four black Protestant churches and one Catholic parish. A membership survey taken in 1926 revealed that 3,887 of 4,777 members of white churches were Methodist, Christian, Baptist, and Presbyterian, and all but 75 of 1,086 black church members were Methodist, Baptist, or Christian.

Columbia's churches mirrored the town's division during the Civil War and the emergence of a free black community after 1865. As early as 1845 local Methodists chose to join the Methodist Episcopal Church-South when the national denomination split over slavery. Other congregations also maintained traditional Southern affiliations. Members of Columbia's churches did not openly question the morality of slavery, but they differed sharply over issues of secession and war. Factions within each church supported the Union and Confederate causes, sending their sons to the opposing armies. Wartime conditions made worship difficult at times, as when the Baptist church on the public square became an army barracks. After the war Columbia's churches quickly restored internal harmony while maintaining ties to Southern denominations.

These churches also lost their black members, as freedmen soon established their own Methodist, Baptist, and Christian congregations. Slaves had secretly found ways to worship without white supervision

Above: In 1845 the Columbia Presbyterian Female Sewing Society purchased— for $50—lot 162 at the southeast corner of Broadway and 10th. The congregation erected this building on the site. Dedicated in 1846 and demolished in 1893, it was replaced by a larger Presbyterian church structure. SHSM

Above left: The present Second Baptist Church building is the third building occupied by that congregation. Built in 1894 at a cost of $12,000, the structure was completed with the help of a $3,000 loan from "Blind" Boone. The building is pictured here with its original tower. SHSM

before the war, but they attended their masters' churches on Sunday. The Methodist church, for example, had 94 white and 80 black slave members in 1853. Several of the churches continued to accept a few black members after 1865, but when blacks founded their own churches, separate public worship became the norm. In 1866 Baptists organized the city's first black church in the home of John Lang, Sr. St. Paul's African Methodist Episcopal Church, organized in 1867, occupied buildings on Ash and Walnut streets before constructing the church structure still in use at Fifth and Park Avenue in 1892. Together with the Second Christian Church (1872) and St. Luke's AME Church (1880), these congregations were important social institutions as well as places of worship, offering support during the difficult transition to freedom, acting as centers of black community activity, and providing leadership in encounters with employers, city officials, and other whites. It was no coincidence that a century after their founding, Columbia's black churches played a prominent role in the civil rights movement.

When Columbians were not working, politicking, educating, or worshiping, they readily found ways to satisfy their cultural and recreational needs. If "culture" includes all of the arts and entertainments which Columbia's citizens have supported since the 1820s, the city has a full and interesting cultural history.

Columbians gathered in an assortment of facilities for edification and amusement. Richard Gentry's tavern at Ninth and Broadway served as Columbia's post office, stage coach stop, and a community center during the 1820s and 1830s. Townspeople and students held dances, dinners, meetings, rallies, lectures, and receptions at several 19th-century hotels. Along Walnut Street at one-block intervals from the courthouse to the Wabash station stood three hotels in the late 19th and early 20th century years. The name of one, the Athens, announced the town's cultural aspirations. Columbians who frequented hotel lobbies, dining rooms, and porches enjoyed them as a focus of the common life. Columbia's court-houses and churches hosted numerous cultural and social events. In October 1832 Columbia's first theatrical group performed in the 1824 courthouse, and Professor Edward H. Leffingwell lectured on the origin of the universe at the Union Church in January 1845. In the late 19th century Columbia's population growth supported an all-purpose theater building which partially replaced other facilities. The Haden Opera House at Ninth and Broadway—which opened in January 1884 and burned in February 1901—staged productions including recitals, vaudeville, and legitimate theater. Amusements like the Chautauqua appeared on the fairgrounds at Wilkes Boulevard. Several YMCA buildings provided space for community gatherings, as did the Columbia Club in its three-story brick building at Ninth and Elm during the years before World War I. Uniting representatives of downtown and campus, the club aimed "to promote social intercourse and intellectual culture among its members." In

Right: A television set would soon replace the console radio in this home, pictured in the 1940s, and join the "funny papers" and other forms of popular culture to occupy the growing child's waking hours. The mass media were among the forces which, for better or worse, deprived Columbia of its "Little Dixie" southern-derived culture in the 20th century. Courtesy, Stephens College Archives

Below right: In the 20th century young and old alike made the automobile a mobile amusement facility. By the first two decades of the century both clergymen and theater managers complained of dwindling audiences thinned by Sunday auto excursions into the countryside. The university and the women's colleges hesitated to allow students free access to cars. However, an occasional daytime drive was acceptable, as these Stephens women showed circa 1910. Courtesy, Stephens College Archives

Below far right: A newspaper account called the Haden Opera House "a building of rare architectural beauty" when it opened. As early as May 1897, "Vitascope exhibitions"—an early form of motion picture projection—drew crowds to the Haden. The largest and most enduring of the Opera House's successors were the Columbia Theater on Broadway and the Hall and Missouri theaters on South Ninth Street. SHSM

OPERA HOUSE

Monday Evening, Oct. 3

THE SOUTH IN SLAVERY

OR THE

Progress of the American Negro
From 1863 to 1898

A beautiful Melo-Drama by and under the personal direction of Chas. S. Sager and rendered by the

COLORED AMATEUR DRAMATIC CLUB

of Columbia, Mo.

In aid of Second Baptist Church.

A genuine cotton field in full bloom
A realistic steamboat race between the
ROBT. E. LEE AND NATCHEZ

Gorgeous Costumes, Special Scenery, and a Grand Chorus of 50 Well Trained Voices.

RESERVED SEATS, 50 CENTS

SEASON 1898-99

Top far left: Hundreds of parades have passed through central Columbia for decades. From the southeast corner of Tenth and Broadway, this is the way the College of Engineering's St. Patrick's Day parade looked in 1942. Courtesy, Professor LeRoy Day and the Department of Agricultural Engineering, University of Missouri-Columbia

Center far left: William F. Switzler and his spouse Mary Jane Royall were at the center of Columbia's social and cultural life beginning in the 1840s. Strong Presbyterians, both worked for the cause of temperance. Switzler participated in the Lyceum's discussions, endorsed the establishment of a town band in the 1850s, and helped form the first library in 1866. He is shown in a characteristic pose, reading. SHSM

Bottom far left: In 1908 at age 44 "Blind" Boone was at the height of his success as a touring pianist. On the road most of the time, Boone spent a month each year at his home on North Fourth Street. From the Blind Boone Memorial Foundation, Inc., papers. Courtesy, Joint Collection University of Missouri, Western Historical Manuscript Collection-Columbia, State Historical Society of Missouri Manuscripts

Left: Amateur theater has enjoyed decades of success in Columbia. The Second Baptist Church raised funds by hiring San Francisco actor Charles Sager to direct members of the congregation in his melodrama The South in Slavery. Social barriers were strong in 1898; to insure a large audience the main floor of the theater was "reserved for white patrons exclusively." The production celebrated blacks' advances since slavery. From the Columbia Missouri Herald, 1898, SHSM

settings as diverse as schools, parks, museums, and billiard parlors Columbians gathered to pursue a richer social and cultural life.

Before they had colleges or received touring entertainers, Columbians created their own social events and cultural institutions. Court days and the Fourth of July were occasions for public celebration in the early years. Spelling bees, weddings, dances, and wrestling matches were among the frontier pastimes that brought Columbians together. Horse breeders formed a Jockey Club in 1834, which held races beginning in 1835. Political barbecues and militia muster days highlighted the summer season for men, while quilting bees and church meetings occupied women in this sex-segregated society. Blacks celebrated their own special occasions after 1865, the most important of which was Missouri's Emancipation Day, January 11: into the 20th century a parade and speeches marked the event.

Organizations devoted to individual or community improvement played an important role in the city's social and artistic life. Beginning in 1830 the ecumenical Columbia Temperance Society campaigned against alcohol and united members of all churches for social functions. The Thespian Society, formed in August 1832, presented popular American plays between 1832 and 1834. In the 1840s the Columbia Lyceum featured local speakers in debates and lectures on important philosophical and civic questions. The many heirs to these early organizations include such women's groups as the Fortnightly and the Tuesday clubs (both established in the 1890s), as well as black fraternal and benevolent societies. A black Masonic lodge functioned in Columbia as early as 1869.

Columbia has been home to many creative artists, among them George Caleb Bingham and John William "Blind" Boone. A native Virginian who grew to manhood in Little Dixie towns, Bingham first visited Columbia in the spring of 1834. The 23-year-old artist spent parts of 1834-1835 painting portraits of local citizens in a studio in the Guitar Street office building owned by his friend James S. Rollins. For four decades Rollins promoted and financed Bingham's career. Intermittently from 1834 to 1879 Bingham worked in Columbia, where dozens of city and county residents sat for portraits. He began painting *The County Election*, one of his famed political works, while residing in the city during 1851. Best known for his paintings of Missouri River life and the political culture of central Missouri towns, Bingham left an accurate visual record of antebellum society. Columbia provided part of the experience upon which he drew.

"Blind" Boone, noted ragtime composer and pianist, was born in a Union army camp in 1864. His surname came from the Daniel Boone family that had owned his slave mother; illness blinded him as an infant. Boone learned to play the piano at age nine in St. Louis while he attended a school for the blind, and in that city's black entertainment district he picked up the elements of ragtime. When Columbian John Lang, Jr., became his manager, Boone began to develop a career in music. His first

Left: Columbia is indebted to its colleges for an endless list of cultural events, including original productions like the Pageant of the Seasons, which these *Christian College students performed in the spring of 1920. Courtesy, Office of Public Relations, Columbia College*

Left: Columbia's schools began offering art instruction in the mid-19th century when Clara Bingham, daughter of George Caleb Bingham, taught drawing and painting at the Baptist College in 1859. The public schools began teaching art shortly after the turn of the century. Pictured is a class at University High School in 1949. Courtesy, University of Missouri Archives

Left: From 1937 to 1950 Maude Adams served on the Stephens theater faculty. Persuaded by college president James Madison Wood to leave her retirement, one of America's most honored actresses passed on to students the lessons of a lifetime on the stage. Adams is best remembered for playing the title role in J.M. Barrie's Peter Pan. Courtesy, Stephens College Archives

Right: While today most Columbians listen to the music of others, usually professionals, it was once common for them to make their own melodic sounds. These students, pictured in the 1890s, belonged to the Mandolin Club at Stephens. Courtesy, Stephens College Archives

concert at the Boone County Courthouse in 1880 earned seven dollars, but during the next several years Boone expanded his repertoire to include classical pieces, perfected his technique, and composed his own numbers while touring extensively. His most famous composition was *Marshfield Tornado,* which accurately reproduced the sounds of an actual 1880 storm. By the mid-1880s Boone and Lang were financial as well as artistic successes; the manager once astounded local bank employees with an $18,000 cash deposit. The entire community took pride in Boone's career, which lasted until World War I.

The colleges enriched Columbia's cultural life by sponsoring visiting artists and showcasing talented faculty and students. Almost any issue of a city newspaper published between September and May since the 1870s contains notice of a lecturer, performer, or exhibit brought to the campuses. Civic organizations worked closely with college sponsors to ensure the success of such appearances. The Columbia Chamber of Commerce promoted the concert of soprano Galli-Curci at Brewer Fieldhouse in 1931 and the Stephens summer theater program after World War II.

While student athletics and social life attract public attention today, the arts and public speaking once played a central role in campus and town life. Early commencement exercises were gala community affairs, as several days of public examinations, addresses, concerts, and operettas made late spring a festival of the arts. Literary societies dominated student extra-curricular life into the 20th century. The university was new when students organized the Union Literary Society and the Athenaean Society in 1842. Before the Civil War nearly all students belonged to the societies, which established libraries to rival the university's own and gave members experience in parliamentary procedure and public debate at weekly programs. The topics of debate included "Is the doctrine of predestination true?" and "Should women be allowed the right of suffrage?" By 1901 university students had organized 17 literary societies. President Joseph K. Rogers and several students founded Christian College's society, the Martha Washington Institute, in 1857. Student Lavinia (Vinnie) Ream, who created the sculpture of Abraham Lincoln that stands in the U.S. Capitol Rotunda, was the Institute's first recording secretary.

Although a frontier town, Columbia welcomed itinerant performers traveling the Boon's Lick Trail as early as the 1830s. At first their appearances were irregular and delightfully unexpected, as when the Fogg, Stickney and Company Circus quickly followed its advertising into town in August 1841. Railroads and then all-weather highways placed Columbia on smalltime vaudeville circuits and brought through town a regular supply of live and filmed entertainment. An Aerodome, or tent theater, opened at Tenth and Walnut in the summer of 1906, for example, to present popular works of melodrama and comedy. The touring John J. Kennedy Players opened the season with *Lost and Won,* a farce which the *Tribune*

Right: Circuses found their way to Columbia even before the railroad did, as early as the 1850s. The circus that prepared this advertisement played Columbia in September 1898. SHSM

Far right: Jane Froman, one of the brightest singing stars of the 1930s and 1940s, graduated from Christian College in 1926. In the fall of 1935 her movie Stars Over Broadway *premiered on Columbia's Broadway and throughout the nation. Froman also spent a quiet retirement in Columbia. From the Jane Froman papers. Courtesy, Joint Collection University of Missouri, Western Historical Manuscript Collection-Columbia, State Historical Society of Missouri Manuscripts*

Left: Columbia has not always enjoyed its fine recreation program and park system. Those who planned the city and guided its early growth neglected to reserve parkland in central Columbia, and service organizations like the Cosmopolitan and Kiwanis clubs took the initiative in developing parks in outlying neighborhoods. Children like these, pictured in about 1940, often used school grounds as play areas. Courtesy, Stephens College Archives

Below left: Fans and reserve players are pictured witnessing one of the less exciting moments in a Missouri football game at Rollins Field during the 1914 season. The first university game occurred on the site of Ellis Library. Rollins Field was laid out by the four Rollins brothers on land south of campus once owned by the family, and was home to Tiger football from 1891 to 1926. From the A.M. Finley Photograph Albums, volume II. Courtesy, Joint Collection University of Missouri, Western Historical Manuscript Collection-Columbia, State Historical Society of Missouri Manuscripts

described as "a side-splitter of the 33rd degree." During its 1910-1911 season the Columbia Theater presented the Helen Aubrey Stock Company and other troupes in such popular successes as *Newly Weds and Their Baby* and *Under Southern Skies.* Beginning in 1907 entertainment entrepreneurs built a succession of movie theaters with names like the Broadway Odeon and the Elite. Over the next decade residents and students made motion pictures the most popular form of theater. So great was their success that movies seemed to challenge traditional sources of authority. Columbia's leading churches campaigned against "a wide-open . . . Sunday" in 1925 and 1929 when theater owners began Sabbath showings. But citizens retained, and exercised, their freedom to choose among cultural attractions.

If Sunday amusements caused controversy, a Saturday pastime generated unprecedented excitement in Columbia. Missouri Tiger football began in 1890 as an intramural activity, but within a decade it acquired features still familiar today. Loyal fans from the start, Columbians gathered at the Wabash station on November 26, 1890, to wish the team well in its first intercollegiate game against Washington University in St. Louis. Two hundred people from Columbia witnessed that game on Thanksgiving Day. Student interest in football was intense; after a Tiger win in 1899 400 males marched on Christian College dressed in white nightshirts and caps, the uniform of victory at the turn of the century. Columbia mayor James Gillespie turned the crowd back at the campus gates with well-chosen words and a revolver. In the mid-1890s merchants closed their stores for some games, so widespread was community interest and so slim the hope of attracting business. Crowds exceeding 2,000 attended some games before the turn of the century, a sizeable throng in a town of 5,000. Whatever autumn Saturdays were like before college football came to town, they have not been the same since.

Games and recreation meant more to Columbians than spectating while others played. High school athletics began prior to World War I for boys and girls, black and white, and townspeople have organized several amateur and semi-professional baseball and football teams as well. The university laid out a golf course in 1900, and 150 charter members began the Columbia Country Club in 1920. Indoor swimming pools at the colleges provided the novelty of winter water sports in the early 20th century, while the New Deal's WPA built the Douglass Pool in the late 1930s. The city and the public schools were slow to provide such amenities as tennis courts, but by 1920 all three colleges, the Columbia Country Club, and some homeowners had built them. Whereas the earliest settlers needed only a hunting rifle or fishing stream for active recreation, Columbia acquired the facilities for varied activities in the 20th century.

CHAPTER SIX

Epilogue: From Southern Village to American City

The descendants of Columbia's southern pioneers, especially in the 20th century, promoted economic growth and population increase, and in the scheme of growth old buildings had little place. New structures expressed a civic dedication to change and progress. For most citizens who felt a responsibility to history, family genealogies, periodic reunions with Kentucky or Illinois cousins, and carefully maintained cemetery plots were sufficient homage to the past. However, Columbians have not made a concerted effort to preserve the structural remains of their history. "Columbia seems to care nothing for its past," lamented Dr. Winterton C. Curtis in 1957. Even in this community dedicated to education—indeed, often to clear space for college expansion—progress has meant the leveling of another era's architecture. As of 1984, only five Columbia residences built by private parties appeared on the National Register of Historic Places, three of which originally stood outside the town limits and thus beyond the reach of progress. Of all the church buildings in which Columbians have worshiped since the 1830s, only three 19th-century structures remain. Most of Columbia's listings on the National Register are private residences, educational buildings, and churches. The remainder, only five in number, are of recent vintage, constructed for railroad or automobile traffic and movie patrons. Nearly all of the city's 19th-century buildings, in short, are lost.

An informed imagination can recreate traces of this lost Columbia. Pause at Ninth and Broadway, for example. Here at Gentry's Tavern stage-coaches dropped off mail and dusty passengers before clattering down Broadway and into the countryside. Here also, a half-century later, satisfied patrons stepped down the Opera House stairs into a darkened street after stage performances. Descend the East Broadway hill, which David Gordon's slaves and oxen once helped westward-migrating settlers to negotiate during seasons of rain and mud. Below the hill in a now-empty field Mark Twain was a guest in the home of E.W. Stephens in 1902. Visit the railroad depots, and imagine trainloads of students arriving on warm September afternoons, or Columbia's soldiers returning home from America's wars. Stand at Broadway and Garth Avenue and try to envision the wooded setting of the 1819 Smithton settlement that stood a short distance away. Experience early 20th century suburbia while strolling up Thilly Street, where in 1905 carpenters built the first house in Judge John Stewart's Westmount Addition. As you drive past Second and Broadway know that white children first received public schooling there;

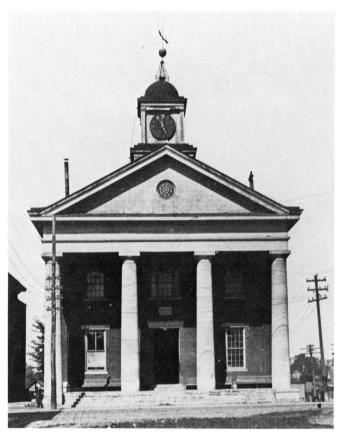

Above: The citizens who persuaded the county to retain its 1847 courthouse columns failed in 1908-1909 to preserve the building itself. Professor W.C. Curtis, who campaigned for preservation, wrote: "one thing that the pioneers to Boone County did not bring along from Virginia was a deep respect for local history and its landmarks." Few besides "outsider" professors cared about protecting the past from the present. Courtesy, Queen Smith

Above right: The James S. Wharton house on Range Line illustrates how community growth absorbs older residential structures. The school district purchased the circa 1898 house with the intention of razing it to create play space for Field School children. But in 1948 Superintendent Neil Aslin and staff "temporarily" moved into the thoroughly altered Wharton house; the school administrative offices remained there for more than 30 years. Courtesy, Mary Brady Biggs

Above: Parts of their past Columbians have willingly abandoned, including the practice of overt racial discrimination. We can only guess why a crowd of white men and boys (and a photographer) circa 1900 would gather at the Clarksburg depot to watch Blind Boone wait for a train. Regardless of his celebrity status, once on the train Boone was probably led to segregated seating. SHSM

Left: The Boon's Lick Trail passed to the right of the Francis T. Russell home at the southwest corner of Third (Providence Road) and Broadway, pictured in the 1860s. Colonel Russell and spouse Caroline Lenoir (probably on the front porch) lived here from about 1850 to 1890. The house stood until the 1930s. Courtesy, Garland Russell

and that the first black school stood at Ash Street and Providence Road. At Eighth and Cherry, at one time you could have stabled a horse or purchased lumber. Near Sexton Road and Providence Road the stately home of a Union General, Odon Guitar's "Eagle's Nest," dominated an outlying neighborhood. In what is now a parking lot south of the courthouse, William Switzler, Columbia's 19th-century renaissance man, and wife Mary Jane raised their family.

Although much is lost, much also remains to delight and fascinate those who would look and see. In the Columbia Cemetery seek out the gravestones of Luella St. Clair-Moss or "Blind" Boone. And in an eastern section of that cemetery follow the names carved in marble to measure the boundaries of the old Jewish Cemetery. At the base of one stone pillar flanking the Elm Street entrance to the university's Red Campus, find the 1840 cornerstone of the original Academic Hall.

Dedicated Columbians have labored for more than a century to preserve and study the documents of local and Missouri history. William F. Switzler was the earliest of many for whom history was an avocation; his *History of Boone County, Missouri* (1882) is a remarkably comprehensive and reliable source for the area's early decades. Columbians Edwin W. Stephens and Walter Williams of the *Herald* were leaders of the Missouri Press Association when it established the State Historical Society of Missouri in

Above: Although these young women are not volunteer fire fighters, Columbia relied on volunteers until 1902. In the end the city decided that only professional specialists could provide adequate fire protection. However, in many other areas volunteer work continues to strengthen community life. Courtesy, Stephens College Archives

Right: Marching Mizzou and queen candidates led the 1948 university homecoming parade as it passed the corner of Gentry Place and Conley Avenue. The event's guest of honor, singer Jane Froman, is seated in the car. Gabler's Black and Gold Inn was one of the most popular student hangouts of that day. The Shack, which served students for another 30 years, is by the tree on the left. From the Jane Froman papers. Courtesy, Joint Collection University of Missouri, Western Historical Manuscript Collection-Columbia, State Historical Society of Missouri Manuscripts

Left: Is this crowd awaiting news from a war zone? No. It is October 11, 1913, and these football fans are depressed by telegraphed scores of the Missouri-Illinois game in Champaign, which Illinois won 24-7. The informal scene is at 107 South Ninth Street. From the A.M. Finley Photograph Albums, volume I. Courtesy, Joint Collection University of Missouri, Western Historical Manuscript Collection-Columbia, State Historical Society of Missouri Manuscripts

Right: The acclaimed American poet Carl Sandburg is only one of a host of public figures to have visited Columbia. Sandburg is pictured playing the mandolin in the late 1950s or early 1960s. Courtesy, Stephens College Archives

1898. Professors Elmer Ellis and William Francis English were instrumental in founding the Western Historical Manuscripts Collection at the university in 1943. Drs. Jonas Viles and Frank F. Stephens wrote histories of the university, while Lewis Atherton studied the economic development of Missouri towns like Columbia. No historian since Switzler has written a more detailed and comprehensive history of Columbia and its institutions than John C. Crighton of Stephens College. Floyd Shoemaker and Richard S. Brownlee of the State Historical Society, Paulina Ann Batterson of Columbia College, the Boone County Historical Society, and the Mayor's Steering Committee to Commemorate the Contributions of Black Columbians—all have worked to preserve and interpret the state's and the city's history.

Community action, motivated by civic pride as much as by the hope of personal gain, gave rise to colleges, railroads, hospitals, and factories. Once only one of several mid-Missouri towns of equal size and prospects, Columbia has become the largest city in the region largely through its own sustained efforts.

Although its colleges have changed, Columbia remains in the late 20th century what it became in the mid-19th, an educational community. In 1969 Christian College became Columbia College, and it now serves a co-educational clientele. Both Columbia and Stephens, no longer junior colleges, offer baccalaureate programs, while the University of Missouri achieved true multiversity status by the 1960s. Columbia's medical facilities and staff continue to grow. At the Boone County Hospital's ground-breaking ceremony in May 1920, Dr. Andrew W. McAlester recalled that in the 1880s the sick would more likely recover under a shade tree than in a hospital. Today Columbians and patients from throughout Missouri benefit from the medical advances of a century in a half-dozen hospital complexes which together provide more beds per capita than any other city in America but one. Insurance, an early service industry, grew to become one of the city's largest employers after World War II. Similarly, Columbia continues to serve as a regional center of agricultural marketing, research, and education, and as a community which welcomes light industry. Long noted for its importance in journalism, the city is also home to several magazines, large commercial publishers, and a university press. Columbia may have more publishers, editors, reporters, and printers than any other city of comparable size anywhere.

When migrants venture into a new land they seek to recreate the familiar. So it was with Columbia's first white settlers, who reproduced on the western frontier the southern society which they had known in Virginia, Tennessee, and especially Kentucky. A century after its founding, in the 1920s and 1930s southern traits remained prominent in this "Little Dixie" Missouri community, like the paternalistic racial system, the virtually unchallenged supremacy of the Democratic party, the religious dominance of evangelical Protestantism, and a slowpaced and

Painter Frank Stack received his professional training at the University of Texas and the Chicago Art Institute before he joined the art department faculty at the University of Missouri-Columbia in 1963. Stack's oil painting of Columbia's Missouri Theater is a part of the State Historical Society's Contemporary Artist collection. SHSM

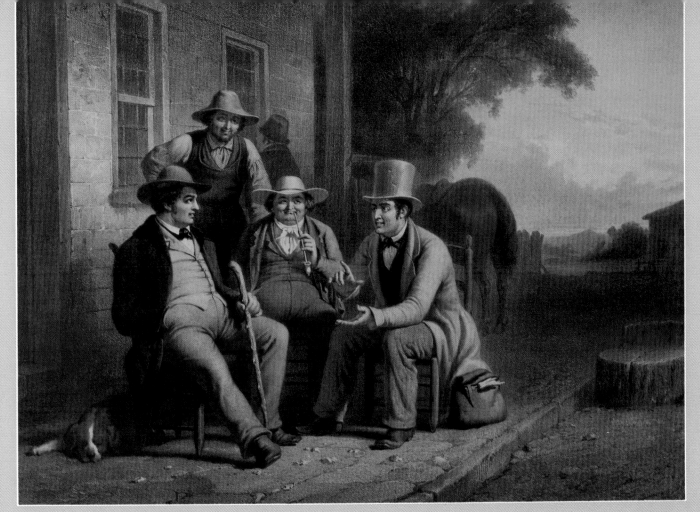

Opposite page: In the late 1930s Kenneth E. Hudson—a professor of art at the University of Missouri-Columbia from 1929 to 1938—painted a series of panels in the old city council chambers depicting historic events that shaped Columbia. Top left: White settlers drive the Indians out of central Missouri in about 1815. Top center: A crowd gathers on July 4, 1840, to lay the cornerstone of the university,s first major building, symbolizing Columbia's foundation in education. Top right: The building of the 1856 plank road down to the Missouri River at Providence indicates the importance of transportation. Bottom left: Columbians celebrate the arrival of their first train on October 29, 1867. Bottom center: The area's importance as an agricultural marketing center is dramatized by this panel depicting men at work in the Boone County Mill. Bottom right: In the twelfth and final panel of his mural, Hudson painted a crowd at Eighth and Broadway on a Saturday afternoon in 1938. Hudson believed that a view of this busy location best represented the dynamic urban area which had grown on the pastoral hunting lands of the Indians after a century of development. Courtesy, Judge Robert Bailey and Phyllis Hardin

Above: George Caleb Bingham rose from the soil of the Boon's Lick region, and his work faithfully reflected its life. A frequent visitor to and sometimes resident of Columbia, Bingham once exhibited Canvassing for a Vote (1852) in his Columbia studio. The original painting is in the Nelson Art Gallery in Kansas City. Pictured is a more widely distributed lithograph of the painting. SHSM

Right: Rose O'Neill, author and illustrator who lived in Taney County, created the Kewpie Doll in 1913. The Kewpie lives on in Columbia as the mascot of David H. Hickman High School, named for a 19th-century businessman who strongly supported public education. Mr. Hickman and the Kewpie make a rather odd couple, but together they help to symbolize academic and athletic excellence in the Columbia public school system. Courtesy, Columbia Board of Education

Left: Drawing upon familiar symbols like those of Christmas, and appealing to traditional virtues like thrift, Columbia businesses sought new ways to communicate with customers. This December 1910 calendar advertisement was an ancestor of the marketing appeals heard today on radio and television. SHSM

Right: Since the 1820s some Columbians have buried their dead in the graveyard located south of Broadway and west of Providence Road. Colonel Richard Gentry, one of the town's founders, helped to lay out the original cemetery, which the Columbia Cemetery Association took over in 1853. In the distance may be seen Jesse Hall and other university buildings. Photo by the author

Above: Columbia's most familiar historic artifacts are the 1843 columns, which mark the site of the original Academic Hall. When workers erected them, Columbia was only 22 years old. The federal government has designated Francis Quadrangle, dominated by Jesse Hall to the south, as an historic district. Photo by the author

Completed in 1877, Maplewood (above left) was the country home of the Slater Lenoir family. Dr. Frank Nifong and wife Lavinia (Lenoir) lived there in the early 20th century. Restored in the 1970s and operated by the Boone County Historical Society, the home is now the centerpiece of a beautiful city park and the location of community activities, including an annual arts and crafts festival each June. The park includes the Maplewood Barn Theatre (left), a community theater company based in one of the estate's original outbuildings. Photos by the author

The Capen Home on Ashland Gravel Road is one 19th-century survivor of Columbia's growth. It is seen framed by the magnificent fall colors typical of October in central Missouri. Photo by Janice Kahalley

Below: Central Missouri's beautifully wooded, rolling landscape provides residents of Columbia and Boone County with abundant opportunities for outdoor recreation. Courtesy, Office of Public Relations, Columbia College

Left: At Shelter Insurance Gardens, a private park, Columbians can enjoy a horticultural bonanza, summer concerts, and this replica of a country schoolhouse. In the original building, the Newcomer School located near Brunswick, a handful of farmers founded what would become the Missouri Farmers' Association in 1914. Photo by Janice Kahalley

Right: Columbia observes each Memorial Day with a ceremony on the courthouse lawn. Shown here speaking at a recent observance is Dr. Russell Thompson, superintendent of the Columbia Public Schools. Nearby are memorials to the dead of two world wars, the Korean conflict, and the war in Vietnam. Buried in local cemeteries are veterans of all of America's wars, including the American Revolution. Courtesy, Columbia Board of Education

The first football game played at the University of Missouri occurred on the site of Ellis Library, in the right-hand portion of this scene. Today Lowry Mall, in the shadow of Memorial Tower and near Jesse Hall, is the heart of the university campus. Photo by Janice Kahalley

Left: A new downtown park, Village Square, occupies a site on Walnut Street behind the First Christian Church in a portion of the downtown business district known as North Village. Fragrant trees and flowers make the square a pleasant place for a game of checkers or a noontime bag lunch. Photo by Janice Kahalley

Below: The heart of Columbia's business district has certainly changed since it was photographed in about 1869. The view is of the north side of Broadway from Eighth Street, looking northeast. SHSM, gift of John L. Pfeiffer

genteel social life among whites that was recognizably southern in character. But change came to the southern village. On the original population base of Kentuckians and their slaves have accrued layers of people who are neither southern nor Protestant, neither American-born nor Christian. The result is a cosmopolitan community. Today's Columbia combines a measure of the upper South with equal portions of Midwestern America and the diversified culture of a college community. The mix is a satisfying one.

Although it was a southern village planted on the western frontier, Columbia was not isolated from the broader currents of American life. From the 1820s to the Civil War the community actively participated in the Westward movement. Its citizens traded with fur trappers, engaged in the Santa Fe trade, fought in the Mexican War, searched for gold in the central California hills, and provisioned emigrants bound for the Oregon Trail. Columbia did experience a certain physical remoteness because it lacked mainline train service. But when other modes of travel replaced railroads in importance, the city again enjoyed a strategic location on major transportation routes, as well as instant access to mass communications networks. As an educational community, Columbia never lost touch with the latest currents of thought in the sciences and the arts. A southern village in the West, Columbia was not condemned to isolation or parochialism by its size or location.

This, then, is Columbia, Missouri: a city of which the tale can be told of a fascinating progression from southern village to American city.

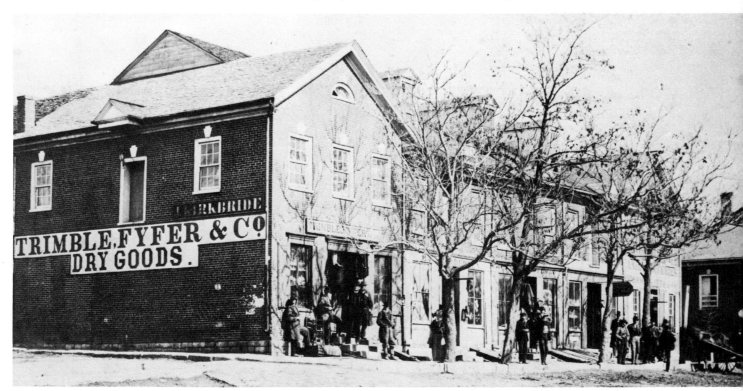

Above: A lawyer by profession, North Todd Gentry delighted in local history. His writings, many of which originated as lectures, are of value to Columbia because he descended from pioneer families, collected documents and photographs, and talked with anyone having a story to relate. Without committed amateurs like Gentry, Columbia would have forgotten even more of its past then it has. From North Todd Gentry, The Bench and Bar of Boone County, Missouri, 1916

Right: From Jesse Hall looking north, this is a view of central Columbia circa 1927. At the far end of Eighth Street only the columns remain of the old courthouse, and in the foreground the university's School of Journalism has replaced the old observatory. By the 1920s some local residents referred to Eighth Street as "Columns Avenue." SHSM, photo by Leon Waughte, gift of Roy King

CHAPTER SEVEN
Partners in Progress

Refurbished in 1983, the columns of the 1847 Boone County Courthouse are a stately reminder of the city's history. Photo by the author

Columbia's economic foundations have relied on three enterprises since its settlement in 1821: education, medicine, and the insurance industry.

Located in mid-Missouri, Columbia grew with its abundant natural water supply. But as time passed, the city's hospitals, colleges, and insurance firms drew more residents and established its outstanding traits.

Today Columbia boasts a population of 65,000, a far cry from the handful of settlers who built a few cabins and wells into the permanent seat of Boone County.

The city enjoys a national reputation, thanks to the University of Missouri Tigers who make it their home and attract thousands of football fans in the spring. The university's journalism school—consistently ranked among the nation's top three—also puts the city on the map.

Columbia is also renowned for its 1,700 hospital beds, making it a regional medical center and second only to Rochester, Minnesota, in patient capacity per capita. The city's eight hospitals focus on treating veterans, cancer patients, and the mentally ill, as well as those who need general acute care.

But the businesses of Columbia reveal only part of the reason people settle here. The city offers an easy-going pace and comfortable atmosphere that relieves most newcomers who have endured smog and traffic congestion.

Easy access on Interstate 70 to St. Louis and Kansas City, each less than 150 miles away, enhances the local life-style. In less than two hours, Columbia residents can also reach Lake of the Ozarks, a major resort area that attracts fishing and boating enthusiasts. But Columbia residents usually don't have to leave to find what they want. As the city's apple-shaped logo says, it's "ripe for the picking."

The organizations whose stories are detailed on the following pages have chosen to support this important literary and civic project. They illustrate the variety of ways in which individuals and their businesses have contributed to the growth and development of Columbia. The civic involvement of the city's businesses, learning institutions, and local government, in partnership with its citizens, has made Columbia a first-class place to live and work.

COLUMBIA CHAMBER OF COMMERCE

James A. Hudson, first president of the Columbia Commercial Club (1905-1910), served longer than any president.

When the Columbia Chamber of Commerce began promoting the city's prosperity in 1905, the main street was still unpaved and the population was only 5,651.

In order to expand the community, Mayor Stanley Smith called a meeting of local business leaders, and nine men were selected to draw up bylaws for the Chamber. Initially called the Commercial Club, its name was changed in 1928.

The organization established headquarters in three rooms of the Stephens Endowment Building at Tenth and Broadway and paid $25 a month rent. Its first president was James A. Hudson, chief of the Missouri Telephone Company.

From the beginning the Chamber's 137 members paid special attention to securing a better train service and terminal in Columbia; as another community service, they raised money to control typhoid epidemics. The group also urged the paving of Broadway from Seventh to Tenth Street because mud was hindering automobiles.

In 1906 the Chamber persuaded the Hamilton Brown Shoe Company of St. Louis to open a factory in Columbia; it additionally helped procure $60,000 to subsidize a local manufacturing plant, and succeeded in luring another one to town.

The city, which began to draw convention business by offering prizes to agricultural associations, found it necessary to improve its roads. Several Chamber members, including E.W. Stephens, R.B. Price, and Jack Hetzler, joined volunteer groups and worked on the roads in 1913.

In 1938 the city instituted a municipal airport, and several Chamber members tried to obtain permission from federal authorities to establish commercial airline service there. However, their effort—hindered by the airport's limited size—did not succeed until 1952.

Highway 40 fostered the development of businesses around Columbia's perimeter, and the town became a center of retail sales, education, medicine, and farming. As a result of the latter endeavor, the Chamber championed Boone County ham.

One of its members, Colonel Robert E. Lee Hill, promoted the ham, which became a regular part of the menu at the Boone County Fair, among hotels and fashionable restaurants throughout the United States.

The civic-minded group raised $60,000 in 1968 to help establish the Cancer Research Center, a private scientific laboratory that works with the Ellis Fischel State Cancer Center—the only hospital in Missouri devoted to treating the indigent. During the 1960s and 1970s the Chamber also promoted parks, expanded airport facilities, and the interests of area merchants.

Today the organization fills modern offices at 32 North Eighth Street and has divisions that work on public affairs, economic development, and other community needs. It regularly offers short courses and seminars on business management topics, and alerts the public about bogus operations, check fraud, and counterfeit-money circulation.

The Chamber also oversees the Columbia Industrial Development Corporation, an organization formed to purchase land and make it available for future development.

Due to its dedication to attract shoppers to the city, welcome newcomers to the community, and to civically serve in every way possible, the Columbia Chamber of Commerce has been an important factor in the evolution of a settlement of 5,651 people into a regional retail, educational, and medical center.

Columbia Normal
Hetzler Ice Plant   Busy Day on Broadway   Exchange National Bank
Elvira Building

JOHN EPPLE CONSTRUCTION COMPANY

The John Epple Construction Company has left its imprint throughout Columbia.

The 60-year-old firm erected the medical center at the University of Missouri-Columbia; it also constructed 19 buildings for Stephens College. Six major additions to Boone Hospital Center that have risen on the city's eastern skyline are a result of the firm's expertise. The Missouri United Methodist Church—a massive stone structure—is one of Epple's finest accomplishments.

From a fledgling enterprise inspired by the son of German immigrants, the John Epple Construction Company has evolved into a regional business that approaches $16 million in peak annual sales and has 80 employees.

John Ernest Epple settled around the turn of the century in Ferguson, Missouri, where he constructed many homes, schools, and commercial buildings. The master carpenter instilled in his son, John Albert Epple, a sense of Old World craftsmanship. The family moved to Columbia in 1928, four years after founding the John Epple Construction Company.

In the six decades that have passed since 1924, the Epple name has become synonymous with construction. The firm is responsible for erecting several University of Missouri dormitories and two wings of its student union building.

John Albert received an engineering degree from Ohio Northern University; however, his training had begun years before. During high school he spent summer vacations and his spare time working for his father. He gained additional experience in the Navy Bureau of Yards and Docks, performing survey and construction work at installations in Norfolk, Virginia, until 1919.

Employed on construction projects in Havana, Cuba, from 1920 until 1923, John Albert returned home to Ferguson the following year to join his father in business.

Two years after the Epple family moved to Columbia, John Ernest decided to retire—succeeded by his son as president of the growing company. The firm continued building facilities at Fort Leonard Wood, Central Methodist College in Fayette, and the Central Missouri State College in Warrensburg.

John Albert passed the operation on to his sons, John Albert Jr. and Robert Epple; the latter became its owner after buying his brother's interest in 1977.

During the past five years the construction industry has become intensely competitive due to the national recession. Nonetheless, John Epple Construction Company has thrived. Inside the office building, framed photographs of the structures that the organization has erected are displayed on numerous walls. These mementos testify to the company's pervasive presence in

The St. Mary of Aldermanbury Church's Winston Churchill Memorial, in Fulton, is another familiar John Epple Construction Company project.

Columbia, as well as in surrounding communities.

The John Epple Construction Company's talent for Old World craftsmanship is evident in the Memorial Student Union constructed by the firm on the campus of the University of Missouri.

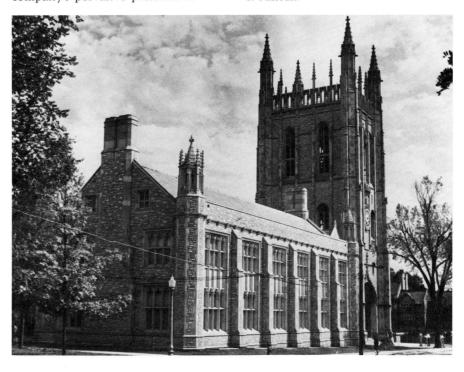

BOONE HOSPITAL CENTER

The history of Boone Hospital Center shows that a health care enterprise built by county citizens can prosper despite harsh competition, fluctuating government rules, and expensive technology.

Opened on December 10, 1921, with funding from a bond issue, the institution has evolved from a 34-bed facility with six employees and 27 doctors to a 344-bed regional referral center with 1,030 employees and 180 physicians. With a $48-million annual budget and a broad range of medical services, Boone Hospital treats some 40,000 patients a year who come from 90 of Missouri's 113 counties. Its steady expansion has paralleled Columbia's population growth, a trend that historians have linked to the city's access to Interstate 70. Boone Hospital's rise has also relied on a group of committed doctors such as Dr. Frank Nifong.

With the help of local physicians the hospital developed specialties in cardiology, oncology, obstetrics,

Boone Hospital Center, located at 1600 East Broadway, is the largest general acute-care hospital in central Missouri.

neurology/neurosurgery, cardio-vascular surgery, and rehabilitation. They kept its emphasis on quality medical care while a new generation of doctors increased the development of outpatient services.

The hospital's inception stemmed from a Spanish influenza epidemic that struck Columbia residents in 1918. With only a student medical center, the city was poorly equipped to handle hundreds of patients and, as a result, many died.

Construction of Boone Hospital began in 1919 on four acres atop what was known as East Broadway Hill, a pretty spot overlooking Hinkson Creek. From the start a five-member, publicly elected board of trustees governed the institution.

In 1932 the facility's trustees asked the staff to curtail admission of indigent patients because of exhausted funds. But a year later the staff commended the trustees for continuing to provide such hospital services to the poor in the face of the Great Depression.

Between 1946 and 1952 voters twice defeated $500,000 bond issues intended to expand the hospital. As a result of the spiraling demand for medical care, the hospital was forced to put beds in hallways and basement areas. In order to solve the space shortage, Dr. Nifong, the hospital's first chief of staff, offered to donate $100,000 for an addition if the community would contribute $50,000. By 1954 the institution had garnered $254,000 in pledges and finished building a wing with 24 rooms. At age 90, Dr. Nifong dedicated the new wing, predicting that Columbia would become a great medical center. One reason for his optimism: Boone Hospital's admissions had more than tripled between 1945 and 1955.

Boone Hospital has traditionally acquired the latest and most advanced medical equipment for diagnosis and treatment, such as this magnetic resonance imaging unit which produces images without radiation.

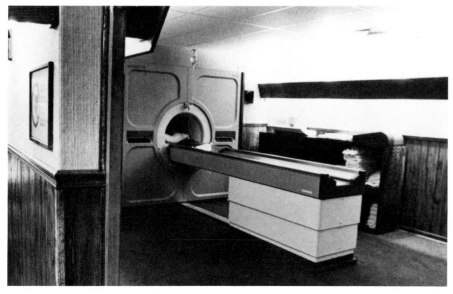

Although a $3-million bond issue in 1959 enabled the hospital to add 165 beds, that addition still was insufficient. The city's population increased from 36,650 in 1960 to 58,812 in 1970, while more and more patients outside Boone County were relying on the hospital. A consulting firm recommended the hospital increase its acute-care beds to 360; however, three bond issues for that expansion were defeated by voters in 1968 and 1969.

The trustees later succeeded in gaining $4.8 million to enlarge and update the hospital's emergency room, radiology department, and other clinical areas. Since 1975 the hospital spent more than $20 million adding two floors, a new ancillary base, and other improvements.

Boone Hospital has traditionally acquired the most modern medical equipment for diagnosis and treatment. It was among the first in Missouri to operate a CT scanner and the second to acquire a magnetic resonance imaging unit — a sophisticated machine that produces cross-sectional images of the body without using radiation. The device helps diagnose cancer, heart disease, and brain abnormalities once hidden from view.

The hospital also houses a linear accelerator and cobalt machine, modern devices that help Boone Hospital's oncologists fight cancer in some 12,000 patients a year. In a sophisticated surgery suite, the institution's heart specialists annually perform more than 450 open-heart operations. Three ambulances remain prepared for emergencies outside the hospital's level II trauma center. Boone Hospital has three intensive-care units for treating people with a wide variety of severe conditions.

The board of trustees changed the

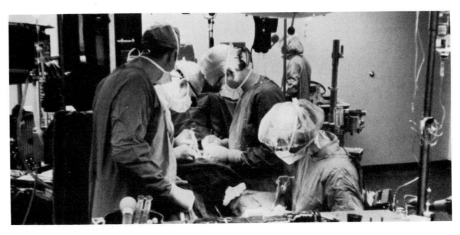

institution's name from Boone County Hospital to Boone Hospital Center in 1981 to acknowledge its new role as a regional referral center. While its mission has broadened, the facility remains committed to the community. Its staff members have developed ongoing fitness programs to encourage local residents to exercise regularly. With a small, wireless "Lifeline" button supplied by the hospital, elderly residents can call its emergency room for help any time of day or night. The facility also screens the public for high blood pressure and other signs of illness.

Boone Hospital's trustees have begun planning a new renovation and expansion project that may cost as much as $13 million, in order to upgrade the facility's laboratory, pharmacy, food-service area, and physical-therapy departments.

Today the hospital relies on county taxes for less than two percent of its budget. It continues to provide essential services, such as obstetrics and pediatrics. More than 1,500 babies are born each year at Boone Hospital.

The first person born there was David Etheridge, whose parents drove through a blizzard to deliver him on December 24, 1921. David's brother, Daniel, was born there in 1924, and both their parents later died at the center.

A Boone Hospital surgical team in the new surgical suite. Heart specialists annually perform more than 450 open-heart operations.

David Etheridge wrote a letter of appreciation on November 3, 1981, that sums up his feelings about Boone Hospital. "The changes for the better in health care that have taken place through the mid-20th century are too great to be described by someone like me," he wrote. "They speak for themselves."

Dr. Frank Nifong, who first perceived the need for more adequate medical care for the Columbia area, lobbied the state legislature to pass a law to allow a county to erect and maintain a hospital. He was elected the hospital's first chief of staff.

COLUMBIA COLLEGE

Religious worship was an integral part of the college's program for many years. A tradition at Christian (now Columbia) College was the weekly walk by students from campus to services at the First Christian Church, as shown here in 1956.

When Columbia College was founded on January 18, 1851, it was the first college for women chartered by a state legislature west of the Mississippi. Christian Female College, as it was called then, was conceived as a sister school to the University of Missouri.

As some historians have pointed out, the growth of Columbia College is a story that reflects the social progress of American women and the nature of this nation's democracy.

The institution fought hard to maintain superior academic programs in the face of declining enrollments and limited funding during the past decade, and through diversification has survived such pressures. In 1969 trustees transformed the college into a four-year, coeducational institution that would eventually operate a coast-to-coast academic program tailored to veterans and active

military personnel. Since then, Columbia College—which now has more students enrolled in its evening programs than in its day classes—has sustained its growth by responding to the needs of the time. In 1981 it changed its mission from providing a liberal arts education exclusively to providing career-oriented degree programs with a liberal arts base. In 1982 the college instituted an exchange program with England's University of Bradford in West Yorkshire.

Under the direction of president Bruce Kelly and a 36-member board of trustees, the institution has attracted a growing amount of private donations. For instance, it boosted its 1974 donations of $189,000 to more than one million dollars in 1981. Operating with a $7.5-million annual budget, the college employs 400 people, including 41 full-time faculty members. The statistics, however, fail to reveal the institution's deep roots in Columbia.

Although many of its founders belonged to Columbia's Christian Church, the name Christian College was intended to imply a broad set of democratic and religious

principles. Some founders—who included three college presidents, five legislators, and five doctors and lawyers—warned at the outset that the college's name would be misunderstood. A continuing problem with its interpretation led to the name change in 1970 to Columbia College.

From the beginning Columbia College avoided a finishing-school mold. Many courses taught there were identical to those at the University of Missouri, which did not accept women until 1868, and five of the college's six graduates were immediately hired as teachers or principals of other schools.

From rented rooms, the institution moved to a permanent home, a mansion purchased from the estate of Dr. James Bennett, a local doctor who died in California during the Gold Rush.

During the Civil War, tensions grew between some of the college's trustees who harbored political differences. One of its founders, Thomas Miller Allen, wrote about the beleagured institution in 1860: "Times are truly tight here . . . money scarce . . . confidence destroyed."

Nonetheless, the leadership of president Joseph Rogers insulated the college from the Union-Confederate split and the school opened in 1861, albeit without a catalog. After the war it benefited from an influx of students from Illinois, Kansas, and Indiana joining those from Kentucky, Arkansas, and Texas.

Today the private, nonprofit college attracts students from all over the world. Its place in Columbia seems assured through strong community support, as well as through its new emphasis on career orientation through degree programs such as business administration and data processing.

SHELTER INSURANCE COMPANIES

Thirteen state flags flutter in front of Shelter Insurance Companies' Columbia headquarters. They represent the firm's growth from a small mutual insurance company that primarily served rural Missourians in 1945 to today's diversified business with 3,000 agents and employees and 1.5 million policyholders.

A multicolored water fountain and a manicured flower garden also dot Shelter Insurance Companies' landscape at 1817 West Broadway; they represent the firm's commitment to the Columbia community. On summer nights the fountain becomes a family gathering place; during the days wedding parties, musicians, and baseball players bring the garden alive.

It all began nearly 40 years ago with a $100,000 pledge from the Missouri Farmer's Association. On July 6, 1945, the association decided to start its own casualty insurance company, and set aside $100,000 in

government bonds to enable the new enterprise to write policies. MFA Mutual Insurance Company (as it was then called) initially sold automobile insurance policies to Missourians who lived in rural areas, soliciting business in a full-page ad in *The Missouri Farmer* magazine. The response from farmers and the general public was enthusiastic, and in 1946 MFA Mutual issued 16,000 policies with premiums in excess of $519,000. Halfway through its third year of operation, the organization repaid the $100,000 surplus the Missouri Farmer's Association had provided.

After sharing offices with the Missouri Farmer's Association in Columbia, MFA Mutual opened a branch in Springfield, Missouri, in March 1948, and a St. Joseph office three months later. Ben Whitaker opened the company's first outlet outside of Missouri in Rogers, Arkansas, and by 1951 expansion into Kansas, Nebraska, and Illinois

had begun. Iowa, Kentucky, and Tennessee were added in 1960; Indiana, Minnesota, and Oklahoma joined the list in 1961. Another period of expansion came in 1970, when Colorado, Mississippi, Louisiana, and Texas became sites of MFA Mutual's operation.

As the firm expanded its geographic coverage, it also diversified its services. Today the corporation offers life and health insurance, as well as fire and auto coverage.

After outgrowing its original headquarters, MFA Mutual moved into its present home-office building in 1957 — which has since doubled in size. In addition, a warehouse was built and an annex was turned into a drive-in claims office.

In 1980 MFA Mutual became autonomous from its parent company, the Missouri Farmer's Association, and with the move changed its name to Shelter Insurance Companies. It also adopted a new red, white, and blue emblem using the words, "Shield of Shelter," as a slogan.

Gustav Lehr was named president in July 1981; he was preceded by F.V. Heinkel, J.M. Silvey, A.D. Sappington, and Howard B. Lang. Through their combined efforts the firm has gained about $550 million in assets and $148 million in surplus.

However, the statistics hold little meaning for Columbia residents, who each year enjoy Shelter Insurance Companies' summer and fall concerts, ranging from classical music to jazz, as well as its rock, rose, and fern gardens, which are open from dusk until dawn and offer a brief respite from the hectic business world.

The home office of Shelter Insurance Companies (top left) is located in Columbia at 1817 West Broadway. The entry is graced by the magnificent fountain shown here (left).

SILVEY CORPORATION

J.M. Silvey formed the Silvey Corporation in 1964 after his discharge from another Columbia insurance company. The meteoric rise of the organization is a testimony to its founder's iron will and strong business acumen.

A Willow Springs, Missouri, native who moved to Columbia in 1938, Silvey established MFA Mutual Insurance Company in 1946; his success there threatened his superiors and he was dismissed. Silvey then tried cattle farming for three months before he decided to reorganize a holding company— which in 1983 earned more than $4.1 million in profits and produced more than $50 million in revenues.

The umbrella corporation owns and operates three fire and casualty companies, a life insurance firm, a premium finance concern, and a finance business division. As of this writing, Royal Group, Inc., plans to buy the organization, a move that would boost the price of its 2,100 shareholders' stock by $17 each to $35 per share. Silvey's nine-member board of directors approved the takeover bid by the U.S. subsidiary of the London-based Royal Insurance PLC on October 26, 1983.

The home office of the Silvey Fire & Casualty companies.

The home office of the Silvey Corporation is located at 3301 West Broadway on 10 acres adjacent to rolling farmland.

The transaction would culminate a year of negotiations with J.M. Silvey, who, at age 74, is president and director of the insurance company. The entrepreneur started the corporation with his wife, Ivis, and son, James, plus 23 employees who left MFA Mutual.

Today the Silvey Corporation has about 235 employees and 475 agents. Most of its business is concentrated in Missouri, Kansas, Arkansas, and Oklahoma. While the firm's shareholders live in 42 states and Canada, the majority are Missouri residents.

From basement headquarters in a Columbia shopping mall, the organization moved in 1973 to a spacious, modern building on 10 acres that are adjacent to rolling farmland. Its offices at 3301 West Broadway are as tidy as a military barrack after inspection. Inside a sparsely decorated, paneled office, J.M. Silvey, who has a reputation as a firm, but fair boss, oversees the operations, and all but four of the 23 people who left MFA Mutual in 1964 still work for him.

During high school Silvey excelled in mathematics and bookkeeping; and two months before he graduated in 1928, MFA hired him as bookkeeper for a local farm cooperative. From that position he rose from a cooperative manager to an auditor and accountant.

After only 10 years of employment with the firm, the young man was sent to Columbia to manage five local cooperatives, start a farm-supply program, and develop an insurance company; he expanded the operation to 15 co-ops with $5 million in sales and $500,000 surplus. The farm-supply program handled fertilizer, roofing, baler twine, and many other supplies.

With business in 12 states, MFA Mutual Insurance Company (as it was then called) had assets of $40 million, premiums of $34 million, and a surplus of more than $14 million, Silvey states. Even with that record, the directors of MFA Mutual fired him on February 10, 1964; consequently—less than four months later—he, his wife, and son incorporated their own enterprise. The 23 people who left MFA Mutual landed top posts at the new organization and shared its stock.

Silvey steadily built his firm. New American Life Insurance Company, a Missouri corporation with home offices in Columbia, was organized in 1964 with capital and surplus of $400,000; by the end of 1983 its assets had grown to more than $16 million, while the surplus approached $5 million.

The Tri-State Insurance Company, Farmers and Merchants Insurance Company, and Midwestern Insurance Company were purchased on September 1, 1964. With their home office in Tulsa, Oklahoma, the group of companies at that time posted $6 million in combined premiums, $8 million in assets, and surplus near zero. By the end of 1983 the combined premiums were about $45 million, the assets over $68 million, and surplus in excess of $22 million. The Silvey Corporation owns its nine-story office building in Tulsa and occupies most of it, renting the remaining offices.

Asked how he achieved such success, Silvey—whose companies have received an excellent rating by Best's Insurance Reports—says he relies on competent and loyal employees who deliver prompt, courteous, and efficient claims service. The astute businessman also remains an active community member, and has served as a trustee of several institutions, including the Missouri School of Religion, Columbia College, and Lenoir Memorial Home.

J.M. Silvey, founder.

MFA INCORPORATED

Seven farmers met in a one-room schoolhouse in Brunswick, Missouri, on March 10, 1914, to lay the groundwork for what later became one of the nation's largest farm supply and marketing cooperatives.

The meeting was organized by Aaron Bachtel, who had read an article by Columbia publisher William Hirth, encouraging farmers to join farm clubs. Out of that association grew MFA Incorporated, an agribusiness cooperative with more than 89,000 members in nine midwestern states.

From modest beginnings—an order for 1,150 pounds of baler twine placed by those seven farmers through Hirth—MFA Incorporated has evolved into a diversified venture that supplies farmers with seed, fertilizer, agricultural chemicals, livestock feed, animal health products, farm supplies, and a market for their grain.

MFA's history begins with Hirth, who published the first issue of *The Missouri Farmer and Breeder* on October 15, 1908. The magazine's goal was to serve as a mouthpiece for a farm organization. Changing the name of the periodical to *The Missouri Farmer* in 1912, Hirth began to urge his readers to join the growing cooperative movement. He realized that a farm organization must enter the marketing field and save money for its members.

In December 1915 the first county-wide association of farmers met in Warrenton, Missouri. Two years later 500 people met in Columbia at the University of Missouri and formally organized MFA.

The cooperative held its first convention in Sedalia in August 1917, electing T.B. Ingwerson of Bowling Green, Missouri, as president. Eleven other presidents served until 1928, when Hirth was elected to the post.

A gruff but kind man with shaggy eyebrows, Hirth served until his death in October 1940. Eighteen months earlier he had resigned his duties to run for Missouri's governorship; however, his bid for the post was unsuccessful. F.V. Heinkel, who had been vice-president since

Boone County farmers once brought their grain to this MFA Exchange, which was located at the corner of Broadway and Providence in downtown Columbia.

Delegates from throughout MFA Incorporated's market territory meet each year at Columbia's Hearnes Center for the cooperative's annual convention.

1936, assumed the presidency after Hirth's death.

MFA purchased *The Missouri Farmer* in 1941 and made it the official publication for the cooperative. Also in that year, MFA moved into a new office building at the southwest corner of Seventh and Locust streets, where its head-quarters still stands today. A second MFA building was com-pleted in 1949 on the southeast corner of that intersection and a third in 1981 on the northwest corner. In 1967 the organization changed the name of its magazine to *Today's Farmer* to reflect MFA's membership in eight states other than Missouri.

Under the leadership of Eric G. Thompson, who was elected president in 1979, the cooperative continues to grow. Today MFA Incorporated has annual sales of approximately one billion dollars and more than $200 million in assets.

MFA serves its members today through 75 company-owned and 75 locally owned exchanges in Missouri, Arkansas, Iowa, Nebraska, and Oklahoma. The cooperative also owns terminal grain elevators in Lamar, Hannibal, Louisiana, Caruthersville, and Aurora, Missouri, and in Hull, Illinois, where grain is stored before it is sold for domestic or export use.

The firm operates seven feed mills in Springfield, Aurora, Lebanon, St. Joseph, Kirksville, Mexico, and Gerald, Missouri; and Monarch Feeds in Dexter, Missouri, and Pocahontas, Arkansas, as a wholly owned subsidiary. MFA owns a fertilizer-manufacturing plant at Palmyra, Missouri, as well.

The cooperative founded MFA Oil Company in 1929 to provide petroleum products to its exchanges. The MFA Livestock Association was originated in 1958 to offer producers competitive prices at nearby markets.

MFA's members are represented at regional meetings and an annual convention held every August in Columbia by elected delegates. The delegates elect two members from each of the cooperative's 15 voting districts to serve on MFA's board of directors.

As membership changes and agriculture becomes more progressive, MFA Incorporated will continue to diversify and adapt its operations to serve the needs of its members and to maximize returns. In so doing, MFA will provide farmers with the products and services that will allow them to produce the crops and livestock that find their way to Columbia's dinner tables as the world's most reasonably priced and highest-quality food.

MFA Incorporated will continue to play a vital role in Columbia and in agriculture, and agriculture will remain America's largest industry. With one in every five Americans employed in agriculturally related jobs, with each American farmer feeding himself and 76 other people, and with agricultural exports remaining the major contributor to America's balance of trade, agri-culture is the single most significant business in the economic and social stability of this country and the world.

The Boone County MFA Exchange is located in Columbia on Route B. It is one of 150 MFA retail facilities. Farmers market their grain and purchase farm inputs at their nearby MFA Exchange.

KNIPP CONSTRUCTION COMPANY

As a child, Richard Knipp built birdhouses, cedar chests, and farm buildings. Later he parlayed his ability into an aggressive commercial construction firm based in Columbia.

Founded in 1945, the Knipp Construction Company has left an indelible imprint in central Missouri by erecting everything from schools and churches to public libraries, municipal buildings, and shopping centers.

The man behind the firm has left as much of a mark through his community service as he has through his buildings. Knipp served on the Columbia City Council for 12 years and stepped down from that role only to join the Columbia Planning and Zoning Commission. The plaques and awards that line his office at 1204 Pannell Street are a testimonial to his devotion to Columbia and the pride he has taken in making it a better place to live.

Knipp can draw up a list of his building contributions with ease. They include the Columbia Public

Richard Knipp (second from left), was a Columbia City Council member when a time capsule was installed in the lobby of the Boone County Bank on April 18, 1969.

Richard Henry Knipp, founder.

Library, Oakland Junior High School, and four of the city's elementary schools. Though nearing retirement at this writing, Knipp still enjoys going into the field with some of his employees and handling bricks and mortar.

A Tipton, Missouri, native, he moved to Columbia in 1940. He first worked in the carpenter shop at the University of Missouri-Columbia. Then he started building family residences, using his home as an office. Knipp never received a formal education, but he always knew he wanted to earn a living in the construction business.

In 1945 he founded the Knipp Construction Company and hired two carpenters, P.H. Barbee and Harold Mitchell. They shared an office with the Heisler Realty Company, at 10-A South Ninth Street.

The firm's first commercial job entailed the construction of an office, shop, and warehouse for the Hulett Heating Company, located at 119 South Seventh Street. Later Knipp renovated Breisch's Restaurant at Ninth and Locust

streets, and built the Calvary Baptist Church at 606 Ridgeway Avenue. Richard Knipp's booming business surpassed even his own expectations; his original intention was to move to Springfield, Missouri, but Columbia's opportunities persuaded him to stay.

During the company's first year of operation, Knipp worked on four construction jobs. By 1984 this number had grown to as many as 20 jobs a year, due in large part to the city's growing population.

The loyalty of his workers—some of whom have been employed by Knipp more than 25 years—also gave continuity and stability to the business. William D. Powell, Jr., long worked as the firm's general manager. He retired in 1982, and Steve Shufelberger took over that key post.

Shufelberger marvels at the energy and enthusiasm of his boss. Knipp rarely relaxes during busy working

COLUMBIA DAILY TRIBUNE

For 83 years the *Columbia Daily Tribune* has chronicled the history of Boone County. During that time the newspaper has left a mark on American journalism with award-winning reporting, design, and photography.

The paper's history begins with Charles Munro Strong, a University of Missouri graduate who published the *Tribune's* first issue on September 12, 1901, on the third floor of Stone's Music Hall at 15 South Ninth Street.

On January 16, 1902, Ernest Mitchell joined the enterprise as a partner and moved the operation to the Whittle Building on Broadway, now occupied by a Chinese restaurant. Shortly after Mitchell became the paper's sole owner, he died in a typhoid epidemic. With the help of her father and husband, Mrs. Henry J. Waters, Sr., bought the business for her brother, Edwin M. Watson, at a cost of $3,000. When he returned from a Caribbean cruise on December 15, 1905, the St. Louis newspaper reporter took over the operation— and began 37 years as its editor and proprietor. A staunch Democrat who loved the spotlight, Watson commented almost daily in editorials on Columbia's basic needs—street paving, parks, and pure water.

Born in Millersburg, Missouri, Watson worked as a reporter for the *St. Joseph Ballot,* the *Fort Worth Telegram,* and the *St. Louis Star* before he took over the *Columbia Tribune.* As a result of that experience, he supported an effort to start a journalism school at the University of Missouri when curators considered the idea in 1906. He wrote: "Many people still adhere to the ancient theory that journalists, like poets, are born and not made, and to a certain extent that is true, but even a newspaper man ... can learn something if

properly taught."

Watson died on November 30, 1937, the day after his 70th birthday. He was succeeded by his nephew, Henry J. "Jack" Waters, Jr., a University of Missouri graduate associated with the *Tribune* as a reporter and advertising manager.

From 1947 to 1973 the newspaper was published from a brick building on the corner of Seventh and Cherry streets, the present home of Deja Vu, a popular dance hall. As Columbia grew in the 20th century, more Republicans settled in town and the *Tribune's* Democratic voice became more independent. Editorials questioned whether municipal improvements proposed by the city council were wise.

Under Waters' administration the *Tribune* added a variety of features—advice columns, syndicated political comment, cartoons, and comic strips.

As noted by local historian John C. Crighton, the paper's circulation increased from 5,183 in 1937 to 13,409 in 1966; its growth in employees paralleled its circulation leap. Jack Waters retired from active supervision of the newspaper on May 25, 1966, and his son, Henry J. "Hank" Waters III, succeeded him as editor and publisher.

Over the years the new publisher transformed the *Tribune* to a metropolitan newspaper that regularly won state and national awards for outstanding photos, design, and feature reporting. Waters

Henry J. Waters III, editor and publisher of the Columbia Daily Tribune.

moved the *Tribune* into new quarters at 101 North Fourth Street on December 10, 1973. With new presses, he began printing surrounding newspapers on a contractual basis, and in 1975 acquired the *Kingdom Daily News* in Fulton, Missouri.

As did Watson, Hank Waters comments daily on Columbia's news developments. One of his friends once wrote: "Hank is a man of definite opinions, owned by no one and a devoted booster of the city in which he matured."

This building at 101 North Fourth Street has housed the Columbia Daily Tribune *since 1973.*

MISSOURI STORE COMPANY

Seventy-five years ago a small group of M.U. students and interested investors formed a company to operate a college bookstore on the northeast corner of Ninth Street and Conley Avenue. That small enterprise has endured to become one of Columbia's leading employers, as well as a nationally recognized innovator in the college bookstore industry.

R.E. Lucas, C.E. Carey, H.B. Kline, W.H. Orr, and Don C. McVay joined in 1909 to incorporate the Missouri Store Company. Carey, who was then the manager of the University Co-operative Store, and his employee, Lucas, were the prime movers behind the new venture, although Kline was the major stockholder.

By 1911 R.E. Lucas and his brother, Boyd, had assumed total control of the company. The two brothers, with aggressive management and a dedication to customer service, continued to develop and expand the operations through the 1920s. In 1923 the Missouri Store, as it was known

The original Missouri Store building at Ninth Street and Conley Avenue in Columbia, circa 1920. Students are lined up waiting to hear the score of a Missouri football game.

then, relocated to larger quarters at 909 Lowry Street. The Missouri Bookstore, as it was later renamed, still operates in this location today.

The Missouri Store Company was engaged in selling classroom and teaching supplies in the early 1920s, as well as classroom furniture and fixtures to all of the public schools in the state of Missouri. By this time it had also become a well-established wholesaler of used college textbooks. Each year approximately 50,000 catalogs, listing over 5,000 textbook titles, were mailed to college bookstores and professors across the country.

The Colorado Bookstore in Boulder, Colorado, was opened in 1930. The Campus Textbook Exchange in Berkeley, California, began operations in 1935, and both these stores remain in operation today. These units, along with the Missouri Bookstore, are three of the oldest privately owned college bookstores in the country.

R.E. Lucas purchased his brother's interest in 1937. Boyd then moved to Berkeley, California, where he went into competition with his brother's Berkeley store. R.E. Lucas continued to expand his company, and in 1941 the operations included a store at Eighth and Broadway (the present site of Farm and Home

Savings), the Christian College Bookstore, Stephens College Bookstore, Colorado Bookstore, Campus Textbook Exchange, a stationery store in Jefferson City, and the Missouri Bookstore.

Immediately after World War II R.E. " Bud " Lucas, Jr., joined his father in the business. M. Stanley Ginn, R.E. Lucas' son-in-law, joined the firm in 1946. In early 1947 a second off-campus retail store was opened in downtown Columbia. The Missouri Home Appliance Store, as it was named, commenced operations at 10th and Cherry, the present site of Harpo's Bar.

R.E. Lucas died unexpectedly of a stroke in December 1947. The following month Bud Lucas was elected president of the firm and Stanley Ginn was named chairman.

The dramatic increase in college enrollments occasioned by the G.I. Bill gave impetus to another round of growth. By the end of 1948 the company had opened stores in Fayetteville, Arkansas; Stillwater, Oklahoma; and a second store in Los Angeles. The stores in Fayetteville and Stillwater were closed in 1952. The Los Angeles unit survived until the late 1970s.

G.M. Schuppan was employed as general manager of the firm in 1947. In this capacity, he oversaw its day-to-day operations until his death in 1978. Schuppan was one of many career employees who helped to make the Missouri Store Company grow and prosper.

The 1950s and 1960s brought about a period of steady growth as the firm evolved exclusively into an operator of retail college bookstores. New stores were opened in California in the cities of Irvine and Fullerton. A second outlet on the University of Missouri campus in Columbia began operations during this period. The Student Book and Supply Store opened its doors in

1959 on Conley Avenue. A second store was opened in East Lansing, Michigan, serving the Michigan State University campus. By 1965, however, both downtown Columbia outlets had been closed.

The third descendant of R.E. Lucas joined the firm in 1959. William C. Lucas, joining his brother and brother-in-law, was elected to the board of directors.

The Missouri Bookstore saw a complete facelifting in 1962. Its three-story core structure, built in the 1920s, underwent a major renovation.

A significant turn took place in 1973. With 15 retail college bookstores spread across the country from Miami, Florida, to Berkeley, California, it became feasible to reenter the used-textbook, wholesale business that had been abandoned after World War II. University Book Services opened its doors in the A&P grocery store building at 310 South Ninth Street in Columbia. Initially, this new division focused on buying and selling used textbooks from, and to, company stores, as well as other college bookstores in the Midwest. In 1978 University Book Services changed

The Missouri Book Store, 909 Lowry Plaza.

its name to Missouri Book Services (MBS) and moved to a larger facility at 1711 Paris Road. The implementation of the used-textbook industry's first on-line, computer-based order entry system was witnessed in 1979 at MBS. That same year this new division's sales more than doubled, starting a period of rapid and dramatic growth that continues to this day. Three subsequent additions to the Paris Road facility have brought the total space to an excess of 100,000 square feet. This division currently employs over 200 persons and is headed by Dan Schuppan, the son of former general manager G.M. Schuppan. Schuppan, a graduate of the University of Missouri with a master's degree in business administration, and a former academic all-American football player, joined the firm in 1972.

Today the Missouri Store Company operates college bookstores in California, Colorado, Kansas, Missouri, and Florida, for a total of 13 stores. The retail division is headed by Kent Simmons. Simmons is a 27-year veteran with the firm and previously managed the store in East Lansing, Michigan, and later the Missouri Bookstore.

The overall corporate operations are directed by Robert Pugh, vice-president and chief operating officer. Pugh is a University of Missouri graduate, a former mayor of Columbia, and has been active in many civic and local governmental groups for the past 15 years.

William Lucas assumed his brother's post as president and chief executive officer in 1984. R.E. " Bud " Lucas, Jr., holds the position of senior chairman and managing director. M. Stanley Ginn serves as chairman of the board and secretary.

The Missouri Store Company currently employs over 300 persons in Columbia and an additional 150

The Missouri Book Services' 100,000-square-foot warehouse and operations center, located at 1711 Paris Road in Columbia.

employees in outlying retail stores. The firm has been blessed with many people who have spent their entire working lives in its employment. Walt Mason served as controller from 1937 until 1971. Roger Williams managed the book operations at the Missouri Bookstore for 49 years before retiring in 1966. Payton Allen managed the school supply department at Missouri Bookstore from 1940 through 1982. Three men, each of whom has over 35 years of dedicated service, are still active in the company today. William Embrey, manager of the Colorado Bookstore, has served for 36 years, F.M. Dick, manager of the Berkely, California, store for 48 years, and Levy Starnes, Missouri Bookstore Frame Shop, for 57 years.

The Missouri Store Company intends to remain a technological and service leader in the college bookstore industry, living up to the motto coined 75 years ago by founder R.E. Lucas, "Ours Is The Trade That Service Made."

COLUMBIA INSURANCE COMPANIES

Mid-Missouri farmers run a risky business that relies on mother nature's mercy. To protect their assets, the Columbia Insurance Companies offer crop hail, and property insurance.

The firm consists of four insurance companies that have thrived on Columbia's central location and growing populace. Tucked into the White Gate Center, the group keeps a low profile.

But the firm's appearance—it does little advertising—is deceptive. The volume of insurance written by the companies exceeds two billion dollars.

Columbia Insurance has 231,000 policies in force compared with just 100 during its first year of operation. The group grew out of the Boone County Home Mutual Insurance Company, which was chartered in 1851.

It has conducted business continuously since then, writing property insurance for Missouri residents. The firm later merged with the Columbia Mutual Casualty Insurance Company, another member of the group.

Columbia Mutual, the largest member of the companies, was founded in Rock Port, Missouri, in 1889 as the Missouri Farmers Mutual Tornado, Cyclone and Wind Storm Insurance Company. Less than a decade later Rock Port also became the home base of the Farmers Mutual Hail Insurance Company, a vital part of the group.

The Rock Port firms moved to Columbia in the 1930s as part of their anticipated expansion. First Columbia Life joined the group in 1978 and Old Western Life in 1982.

The Columbia Mutual Casualty Insurance Company, once named Midland Mutual, writes property and casualty insurance. All of the companies, however, concentrate on rural Missouri, rather than on competing in metropolitan areas.

The group has done well. The firms write more than 50 percent of all crop insurance throughout Missouri. In 1983 they recorded $31.8 million in sales and total assets of $33 million.

The four companies share a common management team that responds to a board of directors.

First Columbia Life conducts business in 17 states, but it does the bulk of its business, like its partners, in Missouri.

The group originally operated out of a small building on South Ninth Street in Columbia. In 1937 the concern moved to 10 Hitt Street to make way for a growing number of employees. Just 15 years later Columbia Insurance changed its address once again—this time to a new building across from Hickman High School on Business Loop 70 East. The company moved to its present site in 1975.

The Columbia Insurance Companies employ nearly 150 people, many of whom work as field representatives. The firms work with 1,000 independent agents.

One of the longest-standing employees—D.K. Seltsam—started working with the company in 1937 as an accountant. Today he is chairman of the board.

Since 1851 Columbia Insurance Companies have continued to grow for the future.

BOONE COUNTY LUMBER COMPANY

Founded in 1965, Boone County Lumber Company has etched out a unique position in Columbia's construction industry. The firm takes pride in the quality of its products and the rapid service it provides to customers. Low prices, while important, take a back seat to those values.

The bulk of the firm's business consists of wholesale trade though it does cater to homemakers and amateur craftsmen. Based on the edge of Columbia's downtown beside a railroad track, Boone County Lumber enjoys easy access to the area's growing land tracts.

To respond to a contractor's request for supplies, the firm dispatches its radio-equipped trucks to building sites all over town. The delivery service is free.

The firm imports wood from California, Oregon, and Washington and cuts it into sizes and shapes to fit customer's needs in an on-site woodworking shop. Much of Boone County Lumber's business is done through competitive bids.

Four men, Tom Allton, Howard Eiffert, Frank Fristoe, and Ray Freese, started the venture as partners. Today Boone County Lumber is co-owned by Eiffert and Freese, a local building contractor.

They started the firm with just three employees, a force that had grown to 15 by 1984. They work at a complex of nine buildings at 1100 Rogers Street.

In the firm's main office, customers can buy everything from paint and modern spraying devices to hardware supplies such as nails, nuts, and bolts. The firm also sells pre-hung door units and other prefabricated items. In total, sales

exceed five million dollars per year. To increase efficiency and reduce expenses, Boone County Lumber started in 1984 to ship its own supplies from coast to coast in an 18-wheel truck.

Aside from that vehicle, the company also operates large trucks for local hauling jobs, pickups, and trailers, as well as four forklifts.

Most of Boone County Lumber's clients are within a 50-mile radius of Columbia. The business, of course, is seasonal, with winter being the slowest time of year.

The firms original building (left) was used until 1982, when it moved to this facility (below).

Boone County Lumber Company is located in a complex of nine buildings at 1100 Rogers Street.

The firm has gone through steady expansion. In 1981 work began on a new main office building bordering Rogers Street. The following year the company acquired a half-acre plot abutting the southern edge of its property. A large storage shed was built in 1984.

Howard Eiffert, general manager of Boone County Lumber, studied to become a teacher after he left college. He received his teaching degree, but went to work for another lumber company—and then started his own.

BARTH'S CLOTHING CO., INC.

At the turn of the century Barth's Clothing Co. treated its customers as if they were kings. Boone County farmers carried home arms full of goods from the store at Ninth and Broadway. They paid their bills once a year—when the harvest came in.

The store's founders, Joseph and Victor Barth, enjoyed haggling with those customers who sought a lower price for their clothing. The Barths marked down items to please their clientele and avoid losing them.

Each customer in those days could expect a salesman to personally display everything from overalls to dress shirts and three-piece suits. Until a customer fancied them, store items were tucked away in boxes, glass cases, and closets.

The store's tradition of individually serving clients continues today under the ownership and management of James A. Hourigan, whose father worked for the Barths for 50 years, purchasing a half-interest in the establishment in 1936 and becoming its sole owner in 1946.

The store maintains another hallmark that has made it attractive from its start in 1868. Its tall, wide windows still stretch around the building like a ribbon and provide pedestrians with a cornucopia of fashion ideas. The displays show clients how to mix and match sports shirts with slacks, silk ties with finely tailored jackets.

The store's roots go back to Moses Barth, who left his Jewish parents in Prussia and arrived in the United States in 1847. From New York City and Philadelphia, he ventured into the country's frontier.

Moses peddled goods on horseback as he rode from farm to farm in Boone County. He and his brother, Alex, later set up shop in Rocheport, a small Missouri River town that enjoyed active river trade

The first Barth store (above) was built in 1868 by Joseph and Victor Barth. After being razed and replaced in 1910, Barth's is still at the same locale today (below).

and traffic.

An 1853 advertisement in the Missouri *Weekly Sentinel* boasted: "Have in store one of the heaviest stocks of goods ever brought to the western interior. Call for we are selling rapidly and cheap. For the ladies, we have a rich and beautiful assortment of fashionable goods of every description."

The store quickly became a thriving enterprise, boosted by the Barths' connections to East Coast merchants. Alex traveled east about every three months and purchased as much as $3,000 in goods each trip.

The brothers sold everything

from shawls, bonnets, and chintz flounces to oilcloth, hardware, and groceries. They advertised a "mammoth stock" and stressed its "variety, quality, and price."

During the Civil War the Barths' store in Rocheport suffered heavy losses from a bushwacker raid. Moses took his family to Columbia, a military outpost at that time. Alex joined the military.

Strife drove customers away from Rocheport and ruined what business the Barths had left in the hands of a longtime employee. On September 7, 1864, a friend wrote to Moses: "Everything excepting death seems suspended and almost every business

The interior of the new building around 1924 (above) and as it looks now (below). Victor

Barth's portrait is prominently displayed.

except the coffin maker has closed."

A month later federal troops burned Rocheport. Moses lost his entire plant and inventory. His later attempt to revive his business failed and he declared bankruptcy. Little by little, though, the pioneer became successful at shipping grain, wool, and other products.

Despite the war, Moses' relatives emigrated from Germany and settled in central Missouri. They later opened clothing stores in Boonville, Lamar, and Trenton. They branched into Kansas and Oklahoma as well. Soon the Barth name became well known in midwestern merchandising circles.

Joseph and Victor Barth, who were Moses' nephews, opened a Columbia store in 1868. By purchasing additional inventory with their profit, advertising frequently, and extending credit to customers, the Barths built a strong business. Today the store stands on the same corner plot.

Victor worked tirelessly at his trade. He bought out his brother in 1906, and three years later added a warehouse to the store. But Victor failed to enjoy the new quarters. The prominent Columbia businessman and respected citizen died on October 18, 1909.

His cousins, Isadore and Joseph,

took over the store in the 1920s and catered to university students. He stocked their "duds." With the disappearance of the horse and carriage and the coming of the motor car "comes a dash and snap to men's styles," Isadore wrote.

As the Barths' enterprise grew more popular, so grew the reputations of its owners. Isadore helped start the Round Table Club in 1922 and served as president of the Columbia Rotary Club a decade later.

When Isadore died in 1936, the Columbia *Missourian* called his passing "a bitter deprivation to the community which he helped build: He cared deeply for Columbia and Boone County."

James W. Hourigan, who had long worked as a salesman for the Barths, bought half-interest in the store in 1936. After Joseph Barth died in 1946, he became the firm's sole owner.

His son, James A. Hourigan, began working at the store at age 17. James and his brother, Joseph, preserved the company's traditions after their father died in 1969. The store remained devoted to stocking national brands of clothing that sold for a moderate price.

In the wake of his brother's death in 1980, James became the store's steward. As proprietor, he enjoys telling stories about the old days when the porter delivered customers' purchases on his bicycle.

But James A. Hourigan also wants Barth's Clothing Co. to stay in tune with the times. In 1984 he added a shop with suits, slacks, and skirts for career-minded women. He also wants to keep the business in the family. His grandson, Shawn, 19, buys most of the store's stock and sells the merchandise on its two floors. Someday, Shawn hopes to carry on the Barth family's tradition.

KFRU RADIO STATION

Jazz, classical, and rock music fill most radio station schedules. But Columbia's KFRU Radio Station, at 1400 on the AM dial, devotes itself around-the-clock to news, sports, and community-service programming. The ABC affiliate also plays America's Best Music.

In the morning, however, it opens telephone lines to local callers. Discussion and debate focus on everything from neutron bombs to babysitters on the station's popular show, Dial 1400.

Throughout the day KFRU, located on Business Loop 70, disseminates information generated by its network of news and sports sources covering news events in Missouri and around the world.

KFRU was founded in 1924. An Oklahoma oilman named E.H. Rollstone opened its doors as a gesture of his patriotism. He gave it call letters standing for "Kindness Flows Roundabout Us."

By the following year Rollstone's financial picture grew cloudy. Stephens College bought the station's equipment and started broadcasting on October 7, 1925.

The station featured music produced by the college conservancy and interviews with Columbia's movers and shakers. During the Depression KFRU's second owner

suffered the same problem as its first.

In 1932 Stephens sold out to a pair of St. Louis residents, Robert W. Bennett and Nelson R. Darraugh. The college retained hours of air time in return for letting the new owners keep the station on campus. Bennett and Darraugh used an old fraternity house on Ninth and Elm streets as an office and studio.

In 1935 the partners sold out to a second group of St. Louis businessmen. After a year, ownership passed on to the now-defunct St. Louis Star-Times Publishing Company, which sent Mahlon Aldridge, Jr., to Columbia to manage the station.

Aldridge and Hank J. Waters, Jr., the former editor and publisher of the *Columbia Daily Tribune,* purchased the station in 1948. The station's news operation temporarily moved to the Tribune Building the following year.

KFRU severed its connection with Stephens in 1950, the year the station's new headquarters rose at the intersection of Business Loop 70 and Business 63 South. Today the station still stands on that six-acre site.

Aldridge crafted KFRU into a community-oriented station, adding more local news and sports. More than any of its previous managers, it was Aldridge who molded KFRU into the Columbia tradition it is

today.

Aldridge was so successful in drawing listeners that KFRU gained the nickname: "The Voice of Columbia." He founded the Missouri Sports Network and lent his booming baritone voice to broadcasting Missouri basketball and football games play by play.

Before his retirement at age 68, Aldridge gave hundreds of university students their start in broadcasting. KFRU alumni now work in major markets from New York to Denver.

At the end of 1983 Aldridge signed off the air and sold his interest in the station to Hank J. Waters III, current *Tribune* publisher. A KFRU veteran, Bill Weaver, took over as general manager.

"Since 1925 KFRU has been like a community fireplace for Columbia," says Weaver. "As Columbia grew and changed over the years residents could simply tune in to find out the latest development and express an opinion, if they wished." There have been a lot of changes at the station since the days when KFRU was known for having some of the best live, in-studio, hillbilly music in the state. And there will be more, notes Weaver. "As Columbia grows, KFRU will continue to grow right along with it."

Mahlon Aldridge guided KFRU for 38 years as general manager before signing off the air in 1983. Photo by Earl Richardson.

The KFRU control room in 1925.

CREDIT BUREAU OF COLUMBIA

As the automobile helped expand the trade territory of Columbia merchants and the use of credit became more commonplace, the Chamber of Commerce formed the city's first credit bureau in 1930. In those early days, one employee kept records on 8,000 residents in files composed of newspaper clippings, courthouse records, and merchant reports.

Soon after its beginning, the Bureau fell into private ownership, changing hands several times until the current owner, Charlie Gibbens, acquired it in 1961. By this time the Bureau's files held over 65,000 credit records and employed 10 full- and part-time workers.

Under Gibbens' leadership, the Bureau has rapidly expanded, from disseminating 15,500 credit reports in 1962 to 91,500 by 1983. Today the Bureau serves more than 400 businesses in central Missouri and maintains files on 168,000 mid-Missouri residents.

The Bureau's expanded resources and increased importance to area merchants is due in some part to technology. Until 1979 processing a credit request required a manual search of the Bureau's 17 file cabinets. But that year, the Bureau modernized by affiliating itself with Computer Science Corporation, a national computerized network of more than 160 credit reporting agencies.

Through additional affiliations with the National Retail Credit Association and the Associated Credit Bureaus of America, the Bureau provides valuable data to national as well as local businesses.

The Bureau's efficiency and resourcefulness gave rise to three "branch" services in the '70s and '80s. The first of these services, Double Check, was designed to streamline the handling and collection of checks returned to mid-Missouri businesses.

Key features of this check-collection service include picking checks up directly from the bank, sending daily acknowledgments to subscribers for all checks sent to the Bureau for collection, and informing check writers with a certified mailing that makes it possible to engage the prosecuting attorney's office if necessary.

A second service, TeleCheck, was introduced in 1984 providing on-the-spot check verification for subscribers. With TeleCheck, businesses have access to a computer center monitoring hundreds of thousands of outstanding checks written throughout the United States and Canada. TeleCheck guarantees payment of any check a subscriber receives if the business queries TeleCheck's computer and receives approval.

The Bureau's third branch service, the Columbia Adjustment Bureau (CAB), is devoted to reducing credit losses through the collection of delinquent accounts.

The CAB's success in collecting such accounts can be attributed to its access to the records of the Credit Bureau of Columbia. Another reason for the CAB's success is its practice of placing a business' smaller accounts with claims from other clients. The increased amount due means a greater effort is expended in resolving the account.

These supplementary services, as well as its national affiliations, make the Credit Bureau of Columbia a valuable component of Columbia's business community. In its own way, the Bureau is contributing to the community's remarkable growth and vitality by alleviating credit headaches for the businesses that have invested in the city's future.

Today the Credit Bureau of Columbia is owned by Charlie Gibbens and is located at 515 Tandy Avenue.

In 1930 the Chamber of Commerce formed the first credit bureau in Columbia. It was situated at 808 East Walnut, where Casey's is located today.

KELLY PRESS, INC.

Linotype machines are still in operation at Kelly Press, offering an alternative variety of type.

At Kelly Press' headquarters facility the newest computerized printing techniques are utilized.

The clatter of old printing machines echoes through the corridors of Kelly Press' brick building at Eighth and Locust streets in Columbia. It is another day of paper cutting, folding, and binding for some of the family-owned firm's 34 employees.

For half a decade Kelly Press, Inc., has turned out printed material—ranging from magazines and books to pamphlets and letterheads—for a variety of customers from coast to coast.

Today the company proudly lists as regular customers the University of Missouri, Columbia College, and the federal government. It also produces college catalogs and colorful pamphlets for the Missouri State Fair.

In the basement of the Columbia headquarters of Kelly Press, old printing machines still grind letters out of lead that later appear in bold type on Tiger basketball game programs. In another office upstairs, computers silently churn out page

after page of catalogs, books, political posters, and travel brochures. Consequently, Kelly Press can offer customers a unique blend of old and new printing techniques.

The business was originated in 1934 by Glenn Kelly, a native of Britt, Iowa, who had attended the University of Missouri-Columbia. In a building at Ninth and Elm streets, the entrepreneur operated a hand-fed press purchased from the *Sturgeon Leader*. His only employee was a part-time assistant from the university. Within three years the operation outgrew its original site, and was moved to the Guitar Building basement.

James Kelly came to Columbia in 1939 to finish high school and help his brother at the printing plant. He later became the firm's secretary/treasurer.

In 1940 Kelly Press established an engraving service for area newspapers. However, the demand for soldiers was stronger than the demand for printing services during World War II. The organization closed its doors from 1943 to 1946, at which time Glenn returned from

the armed forces. During that decade as well, the firm entered the modern print era with offset presses. A third brother, Sherman, joined the company in 1949 as sales manager; he subsequently was made its vice-president.

Kelly Press moved into its present site at Eighth and Locust in 1951 with nine employees. Sales and staff have now more than tripled, and the firm today operates 12 presses at plants in Columbia and one in Jefferson City.

More than 100 paper sizes, colors, and weights are stocked by Kelly Press. It maintains a variety of type-faces for jobs initiated in Columbia —or as far as 2,000 miles away. Although mid-Missouri remains its focus, Kelly Press receives orders from towns and cities throughout the United States. Clattering printing machines can sometimes be heard around the clock as pressmen continue performing the printing service.

MID-STATE DISTRIBUTING CO.

Founded in 1934 by T.A. Burgess, Mid-State Distributing Co. has grown from a family-run delivery service into a sophisticated wholesale liquor distributorship.

Serving 48 mid-Missouri counties, the outlet, at 1502 Old Highway 40 West, sells a wide variety of spirits to liquor stores, bars, and restaurants.

During its early years under Burgess, the firm delivered groceries and other supplies to private homes. But the coming of inexpensive automobiles made that business obsolete.

With a warehouse located at 19 South Ninth Street in Columbia, Burgess hired salesmen and sent them on the road to peddle liquor. The business started to boom at about the same time Missouri legalized liquor sales.

After the state law was changed, Mid-State became one of the first wholesale liquor dealers licensed in Missouri. Burgess died in 1938, and the Moon Distributing Company of Cape Girardeau bought his business at an executors' sale. Mid-State

remains a wholly owned subsidiary of Moon Distributing, a wholesale liquor dealer that also began business in Missouri in 1934.

The initial sales force of Mid-State consisted of three men who covered 25 counties around Columbia. They were backed up by two office clerks, two truck drivers, and a warehouse man.

The firm expanded its service area after Burgess' death and increased its salesmen to six. In 1956 Mid-State purchased the Tallen Beverage Company, a beer distributorship based in Columbia. The company sold that branch in 1980.

Mid-State had to endure changes in laws governing liquor consumption during its early years of existence. For instance, one law allowed any city with a population of 20,000 or more to offer liquor by the drink. In 1950 Columbia's population reached that level. In early 1951 three bars received licenses to operate and Mid-State supplied some of their alcohol.

Three months after the establishments opened, a special election of Columbia citizens voted to shut down these businesses. It was not until another election in 1962 that this ban was repealed, and liquor by the drink was once more

legal in Columbia. Despite the waivering legal environment, Mid-State managed to thrive by selling liquor, wines, and cordials to package stores.

The firm now employs 10 salesmen and 22 other workers, and operates 10 trucks and 2 tractor trailers. Mid-State is the largest volume liquor distributor in Missouri outside of Kansas City and St. Louis. The firm ranks seventh out of 22 wholesale liquor dealers in the state. One reason for this growth is the loyalty of its employees.

Mid-State's president, Elmer J. Berding, has worked for the firm for nearly 30 years. He started as a salesman and became one of those who won plaques and prizes for selling the largest volume of the company's diversified products.

Unlike the days when Burgess ran the grocery delivery business, the firm now keeps an inventory of its products on computers. And today Mid-State Distributing Company imports liquors and wines from Kentucky, Indiana, Chicago, and Florida.

The Mid-State Distributing Co. is situated at 1502 Old Highway 40 West. The liquor distributorship covers 48 surrounding counties.

One of the firm's early delivery vehicles. Photo circa 1938.

COLUMBIA CLEARING HOUSE ASSOCIATION

BOONE COUNTY NATIONAL BANK

Founded in 1857, Boone County National Bank grew out of a mercantile business established by Moss Prewitt and his son-in-law, R.B. Price. They started Columbia's first bank in a three-story brick house on Broadway's south side. At the time there were no adding machines, typewriters, or stenographers. Quill pens recorded the day's transactions.

The bank served as a post office and principal meeting place for farmers. It was the third national bank west of the Mississippi River. During the Civil War, Price took $70,000 worth of gold and hid it in the woods to protect it from pilfering soldiers. He buried another $150,000 in currency beneath a trusted friend's farm.

The bank's board of directors relinquished its national charter in 1864 so it could reduce its large gold reserve. In 1871 the bank regained its charter and became Boone County National Bank.

In 1917 a new bank building opened at Eighth Street and Broadway. The massive stone structure had heavy bronze doors, 10 Greek columns, and a sprawling skylight that filled the lobby with bright colors.

Today the bank continues to grow under the Price family's leadership. By 1984 the bank had $200 million in assets. The largest bank in Columbia, it offers a complete line of customer services at five locations equipped with automatic teller machines and drive-up windows.

Using its sophisticated computer system, the bank performs automatic payroll and bill payments for individuals and businesses that want to streamline their cash flow. The bank's employees also offer financial counseling and manage $100 million in trusts.

FIRST NATIONAL BANK AND TRUST COMPANY

First National Bank and Trust Company was founded as the Civil War drew to a close. Since its start as the Exchange National Bank of Columbia in 1865, First National has become a mainstay of the area's business community.

Located at 801 East Broadway, the bank offers commercial, consumer, and real estate loans, trust and brokerage services, safety deposit boxes, and checking, savings, and investment accounts.

The bank survived Reconstruction and the Depression due to the leadership of its early presidents, Turner McBaine, C.B. Bowling, and James W. Waugh, who left the Boone County sheriff's post to become the bank's chief officer.

McBaine followed in Waugh's footsteps and served as bank president until 1908, when Bowling took over. In 1913 the bank joined the Federal Reserve System. Twenty years later it also became a member of the Federal Deposit Insurance Corporation. Only two other national banks that were chartered before 1865 are still doing business in Missouri.

First National has operated continuously since it was chartered in 1865. Today it is owned by the Landrum family. Joe W. Scallorns serves as the bank's president and chief executive officer, following a term by Marquis C. Landrum, who is chairman of the board.

With 120 employees in four locations, First National operated with about $110 million in assets in 1984, making it one of Columbia's three largest banks.

CENTURY STATE BANK

Century State Bank won a charter in 1972, but it was revoked by the Missouri Banking Board upon an appeal by four other Columbia banks. In 1975 the bank won another charter to operate, five and one-half years after its founders sought permission to operate in Columbia.

The bank temporarily occupied a 14-foot by 60-foot trailer in 1976 while a permanent facility was under construction.

On January 16, 1978, the youngest of Columbia's five banks moved into its permanent home at 2103 White Gate Drive. It was a victory for the 10 local citizens who had fought long and hard to establish a bank on Columbia's east side.

Century State had projected a loss of $60,000 in its first year, but actually showed a profit of $14,000. That was strong evidence that

Boone County residents appreciated its friendly and efficient service.

Like Commerce Bank, Century State is a widely held financial institution with more than 250 local shareholders. As in the beginning, the Colonial-style bank is open extended hours for convenience and has a branch at 1205 East Broadway.

Keith Lindsay, the bank's first president, guided the bank from its infancy to one with $29 million in assets and 41 employees by the time he left in 1984. Don Singleton, a former president of Boone National Savings and Loan, replaced Lindsay at the rapidly growing bank.

CENTERRE BANK

Centerre Bank was founded on September 1, 1886, by two local businessmen, John M. Samuel and J.C. Orr. Its original name, Columbia Savings Bank, was changed to First Bank of Commerce in 1967 to stress its support for the area's growing businesses and industries.

Samuel served as the bank's first president. Orr was its cashier, and Hartley H. Banks was assistant cashier. Banks became president in 1910, and two generations of his family members followed him in management posts.

Banks expanded the bank by acquiring the Bank of Rocheport and the Boone County Trust Co., which was almost twice the size of his institution. Banks' father, Hartley G. Banks, Sr., became president in 1946 and served until his death

in 1972.

Located at 800 East Cherry, the bank became part of the St. Louis-based Centerre Bancorporation in 1980, when H.H. Banks' grandson, Hartley G. Banks, Jr., and his family agreed to sell it, a move that ended their 93 years of ownership.

Aided by the holding company's management expertise, Centerre has experienced solid growth in deposits and assets since 1980. Its name was changed to Centerre the following year, and in 1983 Centerre loaned a higher percentage of deposits to businesses than any other financial institution in Columbia.

The affiliation with the Bancorporation allows Centerre to offer extended lines of credit and a complete line of trust and financial planning services. By 1982 the Bancorporation was the nation's 47-largest holding company with 22 banks and assets of more than $5 billion dollars.

Centerre's officers take pride in producing outstanding returns on assets and equity. The bank's 100 employees are committed to promoting Columbia's prosperity by working for 52 community service organizations. They're not only interested in commercial enterprise, but also in improving the quality of residents' lives.

COMMERCE BANK OF COLUMBIA

Two hundred local investors founded Commerce Bank of Columbia in 1962, making it the

first widely held financial institution in Boone County. Today it's a wholly owned subsidiary of the Kansas City-based Commerce Bankshares Inc.

The corporation acquired the local bank through a stock exchange with local shareholders on December 9, 1969. Since then, Commerce Bank has enjoyed the benefits of belonging to a group of 44 banks operating in 100 spots across Missouri.

The parent organization provides the local bank with centralized legal services, personnel administration, and marketing ideas. With that assistance, the nationally chartered bank has diversified during the banking industry's recent era of deregulation and increased competition.

Operating in four locations, the bank employs 65 people who offer consumers a wide variety of services and products, including interest-bearing checking accounts.

Many of the bank's employees have gone on to become presidents at other financial institutions around the state. In fact, Commerce Bank of Columbia has produced 11 bank presidents in 22 years. Some started as tellers during their college years.

Located at 500 Business Loop 70 West, the bank operates branches at Biscayne Mall, the University of Missouri-Columbia campus, and Sixth and Broadway. In a little more than 20 years, Commerce Bank has accumulated $52 million in assets.

RIBACK SUPPLY COMPANY, INC.

The original Riback Pipe & Steel Co. outlet was located at Seventh and Ash streets.

In 1933 Morris Riback took loads of scrap metal and hides to St. Louis, and returned to Columbia with an empty truck. As a favor to local plumbers and builders, Riback hauled building materials from St. Louis for a small fee. No local building supply outlets existed in Columbia at that time.

Riback soon found himself returning to Columbia with as much material as he took to St. Louis. The idea of opening a plumbing supply business simply unfolded naturally.

In 1934 Riback invited his son, Harold, to launch the Riback Pipe & Steel Co. Harold left a job as an office manager for a Kansas City firm and helped his father build the family firm.

The duo quickly diversified their stock, offering pipe, beams, culverts, toilets, and tubs, and services like welding and threading pipe to local construction workers. Riback first operated out of a building at Seventh and Ash streets, but by 1962 it had expanded into seven structures, totaling 7,000 square feet.

Before the boom times the firm suffered from the Great Depression, when demand for steel dropped and businesses focused on maintaining their facilities. In 1941 Harold Riback entered the Army. After serving in Western Europe, he returned to Columbia as a major in 1946. Just a year later, following the death of his father, he became president of the firm.

Under Harold Riback's direction, the company's assets and sales soared. A University of Missouri graduate, he added new lines of material that attracted new customers. On April 1, 1951, Riback Industries, Inc., was created to carry out the company's steel-fabricating work, a service that addressed hundreds of contractors.

Even with his growing business Harold always found time to devote to civic affairs through membership in both the Cosmopolitan Club and the American Legion. He helped raise funds for community projects and organizations such as the Camp Fire Girls.

A 1958 urban-renewal project forced Riback to seek a new business site. Construction of a 21,000-square-foot building began in 1962 on 5.5 acres on Business Loop 70.

The new center contained a spacious warehouse, a two-story showroom, covered service docks, and self-service counters. In this new location Riback's 60 employees offer customers a wide variety of heating and cooling equipment, plumbing parts, and bathroom fixtures. Currently the firm has outlets in seven Missouri towns.

Inside the Columbia showroom, the walls are lined with colorful murals painted by Sidney Larson, a Columbia College art professor. These unusual works of art depict the industry's evolution, including metal fabrication and the history of the bath. The murals reflect Riback's devotion to the idea that business and art need not be separate.

Though Harold Riback died in 1976, his family is continuing the tradition of service to employees, customers, and the community he and his father began half a century ago.

THE A.F. NEATE DRY GOODS CO.

The A.F. Neate Dry Goods Co. joined Columbia when gas lamps illuminated downtown and horse-drawn carriages rumbled along unpaved streets. Despite the Civil War and Great Depression, Neate's prospered by selling a wide variety of quality merchandise.

Jacob W. Strawn opened the store in 1863. The firm's rapid growth forced Strawn and his partners to move into a spacious building on the southeast corner of Ninth and Broadway.

The store had two departments in 1882, one devoted to groceries and another to clothes, notions, and other products. When sales were made, clerks dropped customers' money into a cup suspended from a wire. Then the cup rose to a central cashier standing on a balcony in the store rear. Change returned by the same route.

Robert Holland bought an interest in the business in 1906, and in 1908 the Strawn-Holland Dry Goods Store moved to 818 East Broadway into a building formerly occupied by Jacob Sellinger's barbershop.

In 1910 Holland sold his interest in the store to Alfred Frank Neate, a native of Bath, England, who

spent his early years in California. Neate moved to Columbia from Paris, Missouri, where he had married Frances Buckner, the granddaughter of Anderson Woods, a Boone County pioneer. Neate's early years were trying. As World War I raged, German dyes that colored some clothing lines became unavailable to manufacturers. Rather than sell inferior merchandise, Neate switched to other popular items.

Customers browsed through a long hall bordered by glass cases full of cotton, wool, and silk fabrics. Ready-to-wear garments hung from racks in a room on the store's second floor.

Strawn and Neate remained partners until 1919, when Strawn retired and Neate bought his partner's interest. At about the same time, Neate purchased the building from Jacob Sellinger and named it The A.F. Neate Dry Goods Co.

Neate continued operating the business until 1932, when his health failed. His eldest son, Sidney Buckner Neate, returned from St. Louis where he was employed by a shoe manufacturer as an industrial engineer.

The University of Missouri graduate faced tough times when he took over the venture in 1932. Banks and stores had folded. But Neate's survived under his

Sidney Neate managed the firm from 1932 to 1976.

management.

In 1948 the growing enterprise required more space. By converting a parking area in the rear, Neate's size doubled. A year later the store added air conditioning, one of the earliest Columbia retail establishments to do so.

The next major move occurred in 1972. Neate's leased the adjoining building on the southwest corner of Broadway and Ninth, again doubling the store's size.

In 1976 Sidney Neate retired, ending 44 years of managing the enterprise. His son-in-law, Kary L. Kabler, took over as store president and manager.

But Sidney Neate still comes to his office frequently. He keeps the same office upstairs. The walls are hung with family photos and memorabilia of his many years in the Columbia business community.

For over 120 years Neate's has maintained its standards of quality and service to the citizens of Columbia and the surrounding area.

The interior of The A.F. Neate Dry Goods Co. in 1910.

MID-MISSOURI MENTAL HEALTH CENTER

Serving 240,000 people in 10 counties around Columbia, the Mid-Missouri Mental Health Center provides therapy for disorders ranging from schizophrenia and depression to daily difficulties such as marital discord and family violence.

Located on the University of Missouri-Columbia campus, the 71-bed mental health center began admitting patients in 1966. It was the first community mental health center established in the United States under a 1963 federal law.

The Community Mental Health Center Act authorized spending a total of $150 million for building comprehensive psychiatric centers. When Mid-Mo opened its doors in 1966, its staff and patients could thank the federal government for $691,000. Operated and funded by the state, Mid-Mo had a $2.3-million annual budget during its first year in business. By 1983 the center's

budget had tripled and its services had been expanded.

Today Mid-Mo cooperates with the University of Missouri-Columbia Hospital and clinics in providing children, adolescents, and adults with short-term psychiatric treatment. Inside the four-story center, Mid-Mo's staff of 300 offers group therapy, individual counseling, and sophisticated medications to solve its patients' psychiatric problems.

The center had an 86-percent occupancy rate in 1983. But an important part of Mid-Mo's work regularly takes place in nine satellite clinics spread across central Missouri. The clinics — located in Randolph, Chariton, Carroll, Saline, Howard, Cooper, Pettis, Morgan, and Moniteau counties — offer mental health screening, evaluation, crisis intervention, and ongoing counseling. Staffed by clinicians who live in the communities they serve, the clinics are supported by psychiatrists, nurses, and other specialists who travel from Columbia on a regular basis.

One of three community mental health centers in Missouri — two others are in St. Louis and Kansas City — Mid-Mo attempts to prevent mental disease from disrupting the lives of state residents through educational programs. Physicians may, however, refer those in need of intensive hospital services to Mid-Mo, where a patient remains for an average of 17 days. Patients pay for their care based on income and ability.

Aside from providing treatment, Mid-Mo also serves as a training ground for psychiatric residents. Students rotate between the University of Missouri-Columbia Hospital and clinics and the Harry S Truman Veterans Hospital, both of which are within walking distance of Mid-Mo.

In addition, Mid-Mo offers ample opportunity for its psychiatric staff to conduct research. Ongoing studies

Dr. Edwin Hoeper, superintendent, oversees a staff of 300 trained personnel.

The playground on the center's grounds is part of the therapy program provided by the child development unit.

Here an aide counsels a child on a one-to-one basis.

are being performed on childhood depression, the mental health of criminals, the effects of divorce, and ways of coping with stressful events.

Researchers regularly publish their findings in professional journals, including *Lancet* and *Science*. Even *The New York Times* has called upon the staff's expertise for medical news.

Many Mid-Mo staff members also serve on the faculty at the University of Missouri-Columbia. The joint appointment enables them to teach and work with other faculty members on research programs.

To control health care costs, the center relies on the university hospital for such ancillary services as laboratory analyses and X-rays. If a patient needs general medical attention, he or she may be taken to the adjacent university hospital.

The Mid-Missouri Mental Health Center, 3 Hospital Drive, serves 240,000 people in 10 counties surrounding Columbia.

It's equipped with a trauma center, a neonatal intensive care unit, and other sophisticated programs.

Though Mid-Mo annually receives about 100 court requests for patient evaluations, the center does not handle very violent persons. They are transferred to the nearby Fulton State Hospital, which has a high-security unit for the criminally insane and provisions for long-term treatment.

Like other state hospitals and clinic chiefs, Mid-Mo's superintendent reports to the Missouri Department of Mental Health in Jefferson City. The department's director receives policy recommendations from the Mental Health Commission, a six-member panel appointed by the governor with the consent of the state senate.

With the help of a community advisory board, Mid-Mo continues to fulfill its original mission by offering a broad range of services. A 14-bed unit is designed for children with emotional or behavioral difficulties such as hyperactivity, depression, and suicidal tendencies. A child-development unit provides patients under age seven with

therapy and diagnostic services.

For patients over age 18, an adult unit offers occupational and recreational therapy, vocational rehabilitation, and family counseling. An alcohol- and drug-abuse unit is reserved for detoxification and recovery.

The center is more like a home than a hospital. All wards have fully furnished living rooms and kitchen units. And each patient bedroom has built-in desks, vanities, and wardrobes. A gymnasium with an adjacent outdoor playground for children is used regularly. A glass corridor connects the center with the adjacent university hospital and medical school. They all blend architecturally, signifying their underlying unity.

Since its inception, the center has had six superintendents, all of whom were physicians. Together they built an institution that had a unique distinction in 1983: Mid-Missouri Mental Health Center was the only state facility certified by the Joint Commission on Accreditation of Hospitals as a community mental health center and as a psychiatric hospital.

CLEEK'S APPLIANCE AND CARPET

Cleek's Appliance and Carpet is one of mid-Missouri's largest retail outlets for televisions, appliances, and floor covering. But the store owner, John Cleek, pays as much attention to family traditions and the Columbia community as he does to business. Perhaps the Cleek family's most publicized tradition is predicting the scores of all Missouri football games in the store's windows. Founder Clifton Elmo Cleek, known as "Missouri 'Mo," was the originator of the idea, which has been carried on by his son, John, known by all as "Tiger John."

Elmo Cleek handed down more than an enthusiasm for sports. His desire to succeed overcame his lack of capital as he built a successful business, important lessons that John learned well.

A Bonne Terre, Missouri, native, Elmo Cleek moved to Columbia in 1947 to attend the university. He wanted to augment two years of junior college education, but ran out of money at age 26.

In 1950 Elmo and his wife, Wilma, operated a furnace sales and installation business out of their garage. Shortly afterwards he worked as a furniture salesman and quickly excelled in generating revenues.

Located in a rented corner of Wilson's Wholesale Meat Company, Cleek's Appliance and Food Service opened in 1956. They sold frozen meat and freezers by arranging financing for their customers.

With $1,500 cash on hand, they moved their fledgling firm to the front half of a building at 1000 West Broadway in 1959. Cleek's inventory now included televisions as well as major appliances. In 1961 Wilma Cleek gave up her duties at the store to care for their infant daughter. In 1962 Elmo Cleek remodeled the store into a 2,000-square-foot showroom. At that time John did little more than help clean up the store and wash windows. During high school he started working for his father as a salesman on a part-time basis. Father and son often stayed up until midnight talking about the day's trade.

"By the time I was 18 there was only one better salesman, and that was my dad," John says. Working for salary plus commission, John spent long hours at the store to help put himself through college. In 1972 he graduated with a bachelor's degree in business and personnel management from the university.

On August 15, 1973, the Cleeks moved their enterprise to a 5,300-square-foot building at 1000 West Worley. Cleek expanded his inventory by offering a wider variety of appliances and a carpet showroom. Of course, "Missouri 'Mo" continued forecasting scores in his store windows. "It just became a tradition," John says.

Elmo Cleek died on November 19, 1973, in an airplane crash. He was 50 years old. "When my dad died, I was scared to death," John recalls. "I lost my best friend, my father, and my boss."

John was forced to take over the family's business during the Arab oil embargo and hard economic times. He drew upon sales experience that started at the age of 15. And he relied on his father's standards.

The business thrived in later years, and John added 1,500 square feet of showroom space in 1977. During the Christmas season in 1981 and 1982, John's young son, John Jr., started selling video games and cartridges. "I would love to see 'Tiger John Jr.' continue the Cleek traditions," John says.

"Tiger John" enjoying a 21-10 Missouri upset over Nebraska in 1974. The victory was a high point of the 7-4 season.

"Missouri 'Mo" celebrating Missouri's upset victory over Notre Dame in 1972. The actual score was 30-26 but 'Mo was unconcerned as the previous week Nebraska had "squeaked" by the Tigers 62-0.

COLUMBIA PUBLIC SCHOOL DISTRICT

When the Columbia Public School District was organized on January 7, 1873, it provided instruction for approximately 340 students. Today the district serves more than 11,000 students residing in a 200-square-mile area of Boone County. Earlier, subscription schools and private academies had provided for the educational needs of the children.

The first public school building was constructed in 1881 at the corner of Rogers and Eighth streets. The first high school building was erected on the same site. Twelve years later a Columbia board of education opened a new high school building, now the original wing of Jefferson Junior High School. In 1925 the district decided to construct a new high school, David H. Hickman High School, on the old fairground site where Barnum and Bailey once pitched their circus tents. Rock Bridge Senior High School was completed in 1973.

The district's early growth reflected the steady increase in Columbia's population. School enrollment doubled between 1950 and 1960, and again between 1960 and 1970. The school system currently includes 16 elementary schools, three junior high schools, two senior high schools, a career center, and an alternative school. Some 1,200 staff members, including approximately 800 teachers, are employed by the district, making it Columbia's fifth-largest employer.

The curriculum of the Columbia Public School District is designed to provide for the general education of all students as well as for the unique needs and interests of each student. Great emphasis has been placed on the basic skills such as reading, writing, and mathematics. In addition, the district offers a comprehensive curriculum designed to provide an appropriate educational program to students of

The first Columbia public school building, built in 1881. Courtesy of the State Historical Society of Missouri.

vastly different abilities and interests as well as rates and styles of learning. The success of the district's academic program is demonstrated by the high scores students make on standardized achievement tests. Annual studies indicate the average scores for the Columbia School District's students are well above national averages. Between 60 and 70 percent of the graduating seniors enroll in colleges and universities throughout the United States each year.

In addition to the general academic curriculum, extensive programs in the areas of fine arts, practical arts, physical education, and vocational education are provided. These programs, together with the general academic program, are enriched by comprehensive and well-developed offerings of extracurricular activities in all schools.

Counseling and other special services assist students in self-understanding, career planning, decision making, and improving their capacity to cope with changes, new ideas, and different situations.

Special-education services are an integral part of the Columbia Public Schools instructional program. Vocational and continuing education are also viable parts of the educational program. Students from four participating high schools are offered more than 20 occupational programs at the Columbia Area Career Center.

The school district's adult and vocational educational programs and staffs have received state and national recognition for excellence. Course selection is extensive, and participation has increased dramatically during the past two decades. More than 2,000 students annually enroll in approximately 500 courses offered in the Adult Education Program.

Good schools are a tradition in Columbia, and that tradition is enhanced through the cooperative relationships that bind the community, the parents, and the schools.

STEPHENS COLLEGE

Historic Senior Hall, erected in the 1840s, was the first building at Stephens College and is now listed on the National Register of Historic Places.

Since its founding in 1833, Stephens College has grown into a progressive educational institution that attracts more than 1,100 students from the United States and 14 foreign countries.

Established as the Columbia Female Academy, the college initially enrolled 25 students who each paid $10 per term. The students studied grammar, history, and mathematics in preparation for becoming educated wives and mothers. In the 19th century few other opportunities were available to women in Columbia. The academy accepted pupils over the age of 12, and focused on finishing their manners and social etiquette.

Renamed the Columbia Baptist Female College in 1856, the school carried on its innovative educational tradition under a succession of presidents, most of whom were Baptist ministers. A merchant and curator named James L. Stephens heavily endowed the college in the early 1870s, and the institution was renamed in his honor.

Under James Madison Wood's leadership, the college severed its ties with the Missouri Baptist Association and gained accreditation as a junior college in 1913. Its enrollment increased from 156 in 1912 to 2,200 in 1948.

By then the campus encompassed 250 acres and more than 35 buildings located on Columbia's east side. The institution built a riding arena and stable, laying the foundation for its leading reputation in equestrian science.

Today Stephens College offers liberal arts, fine and performing arts, and career programs such as sports communications, fashion design and merchandising, theater, and child development. The varied curriculum drew praise in 1983 when the institution was ranked by a *U.S. News & World Report* poll of college and university presidents as a leader among smaller comprehensive universities west of the Mississippi River.

The college offers majors and minors through more than 18 departments and programs. An accelerated baccalaureate degree program was initiated in 1973 to permit students to graduate in three years, including two summer sessions.

Stephens College Without Walls provides an accredited liberal arts program, which leads to degrees for men and women age 23 and older who study off campus. Since 1971 more than 700 people have earned degrees through this program.

The college's 40,000 graduates include authors, artists, performers, fashion designers, and business executives, and they visit the campus throughout the year to share their experiences with both faculty and students.

As enrollment climbed the campus has grown to its present 325 acres. The solar-heated Visitors' Center was built in 1979 with a grant from the U.S. Department of Energy. The Macklanburg Playhouse, which replaces a theater destroyed by fire in 1980, was built in 1984.

During the past 10 years the college endowment has more than doubled, increasing from $4.5 million to $10 million. Patsy H. Sampson, the first female president of Stephens College, is confident the institution will thrive by turning out more professional sports commentators, fashion designers, and other specialists.

The four-story, solar-heated Visitors' Center houses the admissions office and rooms for official guests of the college. Construction of the building was made possible by a gift from Stephens alumni Alyce Roberts (1940), and her daughter, Sallie Franklin Cheatham (1976), of Portland, Oregon. A Department of Energy grant funded the active solar system.

TIGER HOTEL

The Tiger Hotel has been a landmark on the Columbia skyline since 1928. Listed on the National Register of Historic Places, the hotel facade features beaux arts architecture.

The art deco interior, including a grand ballroom, attracts clientele from all over the United States. The nearby University of Missouri-Columbia is a frequent user of conference halls and lodging accommodations at the hotel.

Upon its opening on November 15, 1928, local newspapers praised the new hotel's ballroom, which seated 380. Columbia had never seen such a large lodging and meeting facility. Local businessmen lauded the hotel in a newspaper ad, proclaiming that the Tiger provided proof that Columbia was becoming an "up-to-date little city." The elite turned out in large numbers to attend the opening celebration.

Flowers from well-wishers filled the lobby of the 10-story hotel at 23 South Eighth Street, where it stands today. Several Columbia investors, including J.E. Gilespie, B.D. Simon, and W.C. Bowling, raised more than $500,000 to erect the facility.

The Simon Construction Company built the hotel, Alonzo H. Gentry designed it, and St. Louis and Kansas City banking interests provided financing. Thirty reservations for banquets, dances, and club meetings filled the hotel schedule before its opening.

Though stockholders owned the Tiger, the Sweet Hotel Company operated the 131-room building until 1943. A Rolla hotel and theater operator, Rowe E. Carney, and MFA Insurance Co. then purchased the building.

The new owners held the Tiger for only two months because Shelter dropped its plans to convert the hotel into an office building. Earl Moulder, whose family owned and operated several midwestern hotels, bought the Tiger for an undisclosed sum.

The Tiger remained under the control of the Moulder family until 1965. Louis Shelburne, who had managed it since 1958, then bought the hotel. Shelburne brought with him experience as manager of the Cotton Boll Hotel in Kennett and as past president of the Missouri Hotel Association. As Tiger's manager, Shelburne added a parking garage, air conditioning, an outdoor swimming pool, and a new elevator to the building.

When he retired in 1983, Shelburne sold the hotel to Tiger Investments, a limited partnership of Columbia residents. They had decided to buy the hotel to restore its original prominence. The group refurbished the hotel lobby and mezzanine, converted the top floor into a cocktail lounge and private club, and upgraded guest rooms on several floors.

The new owners plan to improve the Tiger while maintaining its historic and architectural value. Dining room china from the hotel's early period stands on display today. Golden tiger heads and colorful stripes adorn columns in the hotel lobby. Stained-glass lamps light the cavernous entrance way. The ballroom's wooden floor maintains a sheen, and crystal chandeliers hang above the dining room and dance hall.

Large red letters still loom atop the old hotel, telling new generations of residents and travelers that Columbia is the home of the Tiger.

The Tiger Hotel, a landmark on the Columbia skyline since 1928, is listed on the National Register of Historic Places.

CHRONOLOGY

1818 In November the Smithton Company purchases the land on which it will found the settlement of Smithton (in the spring of 1819).

1820 The Missouri Territorial Legislature creates Boone County on November 16.

1821 The first county court session meets on February 19 at Gentry's Tavern in Smithton ● The first circuit court session convenes on April 2 under a tree at Smithton ● On April 7 Columbia becomes the Boone County seat.

1823 Baptists organize the first religious congregation in Columbia on November 22.

1824 Boone County builds its first courthouse in Columbia.

1826 The Boone County Court incorporates the city of Columbia on November 7.

1830 Columbia acquires its first newspaper, the *Missouri Intelligencer.*

1831 An August 9 mass meeting adopts plans to found what would become Christian College ● The county hangs its first convicted murderer on December 13.

1832 Volunteers leave on May 9 to serve in the Black Hawk War ● In May citizens found the Literary Society "for the purpose of moral and intellectual improvement" ● On September 19 Washington Irving spends the night at Thomas Selby's Tavern at Eighth and Broadway ● Amateur actors organize the Thespian Society in December.

1833 Presbyterians build the first church building in Columbia ● An August 24 citizens' meeting discusses the establishment of a girls' academy; the Columbia Female Academy begins classes in the fall.

1834 The first session of Columbia's district (public) school begins on January 20, meeting in the Columbia College building.

1835 Columbia holds the first agricultural fair in Missouri on October 16-17.

1836 Officials erect Columbia's first public school building.

1837 Richard Gentry's Boone County volunteers depart for the Seminole War in Florida on October 6.

1838 Ann Hawkins Gentry becomes Columbia's postmaster and one of the first female postmasters in the nation.

1839 The legislature awards the state university to Columbia on June 24.

1840 The state Whig convention meets from June 18 to 20 in Rocheport; Abraham Lincoln attends the meeting and (according to legend) visits Mary Todd in Columbia ● On July 4 citizens observe the cornerstone-laying ceremony for the university's Academic Hall.

1841 On April 14 the university's first session begins under the presidency of John Hiram Lathrop.

1842 Editor William F. Switzler renames his newspaper the *Missouri Statesman* in December.

1843 Officials hang two slaves, Henry and America, on June 10 before a crowd of 2,000 for the murder of Hiram Beasley ● Columbians dedicate Academic Hall on July 4.

1845 The Missouri Methodist Conference, meeting in Columbia in October, votes to align with Southern Methodists.

1846 On July 20 the Boone Guards leave Columbia for service in the Mexican War under the command of Captain Samuel H. McMillan.

1847 Officials dedicate the new courthouse on November 22.

1848 James S. Rollins becomes the Whig candidate for governor.

1849 Nearly 150 residents of Boone County depart for the California gold fields in April ● On November 21 a mass meeting hears plans for a woman's college (Christian College opens on April 7, 1851).

1851 In May free black John Lang opens a butcher shop in the public market, the first such business in Columbia.

1853 The Boone County Court on May 10 appropriates $5,000 to aid construction of the plank road to Providence ● On June 14 the Columbia board of trustees purchases one dozen buckets, two ladders, and one hook with which to fight fires.

1855 A mass meeting at the fairgrounds on June 2 approves the Kansas-Nebraska Act, condemns abolitionism and "free soil," and reaffirms loyalty to the Union.

1856 Supporters found the Baptist Female College in the spring; the

school opens in the autumn. The Oliver Parker house on East Broadway is also purchased as a campus site ● Moss Prewitt and James H. Parker open Columbia's first bank in April ● On August 24 Columbia enjoys its first daily mail service to Jefferson City.

1858 Patrons form the Columbia Library Association on November 29.

1861 Judge P.H. McBride presides over a Southern rights meeting on April 20 following the firing on Fort Sumter, South Carolina ● Judge James McConathy presides over a Union meeting on May 6. ● James S. Rollins is elected to Congress in November.

1862 On January 2 Merrill's Horse, a Union cavalry unit, occupies Columbia; many citizens refuse to take an oath of allegiance to the Union and post bond ● The university, its main building occupied by troops and its enrollment reduced by wartime conditions, closes its doors in March ● On August 13 a Confederate band led by Young Purcell raids Columbia ● General Odon Guitar establishes the headquarters of the Ninth Military District of the Enrolled Militia in Columbia in December.

1864 Rocheport merchant Moses Barth opens a dry goods store in Columbia.

1864-1865 In winter, as slavery disintegrates, 30 blacks die in Columbia of starvation and exposure.

1865 Columbia blacks establish an "African Court" in January to settle disputes among the freedmen ● An April 22 public meeting adopts resolutions on the death of Abraham Lincoln ● Black Baptists and Methodists raise money during the summer to purchase a site for a church ● The university president's home burns to the ground on November 26; a new structure is completed in 1876.

1866 Baptists organize Columbia's first black church and school.

1867 On March 11 the legislature appropriates the first state funds for support of the university ● Columbia obtains its first rail service, a branch line of the North Missouri Railroad from Centralia, on October 29.

1868 The University of Missouri admits women students.

1870 The Columbia Baptist Female

College takes the name Stephens College ● The legislature locates the state agricultural college in Columbia ● Edwin W. Stephens becomes editor of the *Boone County Journal,* which he names the *Herald* in 1871.

1872 The School of Law opens at the university on October 9.

1873 The College of Medicine opens at the university ● On January 4 voters select the district's first school board.

1874 Columbia native Charles Henry Hardin becomes Missouri's first Democratic governor since the Civil War.

1875 In February citizens organize a volunteer fire company, and the city purchases its first fire engine.

1880 "Blind" Boone performs his first concert at the courthouse.

1881 Columbians dedicate the new public school building, located at Eighth and Rogers streets, on December 19.

1882 On December 12 electricity first lights the university.

1884 Theatergoers celebrate the formal opening of the Haden Opera House on January 18.

1885 Christian College establishes a conservatory of music.

1887 General Lew Wallace, author of *Ben Hur,* lectures in Columbia on May 13.

1888 On June 9 Columbia votes dry by a margin of 468 to 316.

1889 In August Austin L. McRae establishes a government weather station (in 1890 he coaches the first university football team) ● Walter Williams becomes editor of the *Herald* in November ● Citizens gather in a Jefferson Davis memorial meeting on December 11.

1890 On November 18 voters approve issuing bonds for a water and light plant, a proposal later blocked by court injunction.

1891 Richard Henry Jesse becomes university president in June.

1892 On January 9 fire destroys Academic Hall; university classes relocate in the courthouse, churches, and other buildings ● Boone County pledges $50,000 for reconstruction of the university in Columbia in March ● On July 15 Columbia votes wet, 487 to 331.

1893 Investors establish the Columbia Water and Light Company to improve fire protection and provide electricity: electric lights illuminate Columbia's streets for the first time on July 13 ● After the death of her husband in November, Luella St. Clair becomes president of Christian College.

1895 Columbia's first high school opens in September at Eighth and Rogers streets.

1896 William Jennings Bryan attends a banquet at the Powers House hotel during his Presidential campaign.

1898 Columbia's black school takes the name of abolitionist Frederick Douglass.

1901 In October Columbia acquires its first hospital, Parker Memorial, built on the university campus.

1904 On February 28 voters authorize construction of a municipally owned water and light plant in the northeast part of the city.

1905 Edwin M. Watson takes over the *Columbia Daily Tribune* on December 15 ● A June 16 meeting chaired by Mayor Stanley Smith and Edwin W. Stephens organizes the Columbia Commercial Club ● W.B. West brings the first automobile to Columbia in June ● Columbia High School organizes its first athletic teams.

1906-1907 The Hamilton-Brown Shoe Company of St. Louis locates a factory in Columbia.

1908 Columbia journalist Walter Williams becomes dean of the world's first journalism school at the university.

1909 In June the county completes and dedicates the present courthouse and demolishes the 1847 building, except for its columns.

1911 On October 17 the city council passes its first ordinance regulating the use of automobiles, setting the downtown speed limit at 8 m.p.h.

1912 James Madison Wood becomes president of Stephens College on June 1 ● On November 16 the Columbia Equal Suffrage Association holds its first meeting.

1914-1916 The university constructs a new library east of the campus.

1916 T.C. Hall builds the Hall Theater, which in the late 1920s becomes the first in the city and fourth in the state

to show "talkies."

1917 In January William Hirth founds the Missouri Farmers' Association, with headquarters in Columbia ● On August 14 a crowd of 2,000 at the Katy station observes the departure of Company F for service in the First World War.

1918 The influenza epidemic causes scores of deaths in Columbia.

1919 All but one of Columbia's public school teachers threaten to resign in protest of their low salaries.

1921 Boone County Hospital opens. Doctors Andrew W. McAlester and Frank G. Nifong perform the first surgery on December 15.

1922 On August 1 the State Highway Commission selects a route for the cross-state highway, deciding to run it through Columbia ● In May, less than two years after the inauguration of regular programming on radio, Columbia opens station WAAN.

1924 The Allton brothers locate an airfield northwest of town.

1925 On March 19 the board of education agrees to buy the old fairgrounds from David Hickman's estate as the site of a new high school, which opens in 1927 ● On December 8 Columbia voters defeat a proposal to adopt the city manager form of government.

1928 On February 7 voters reject a proposal to build a city hall.

1930 Walter Williams becomes university president on April 5.

1931 Hard hit by the Depression, the Hamilton-Brown Shoe Company closes its factory in January.

1932 Columbia erects both the city hall at Sixth and Broadway and the fire and police building at Seventh and Walnut.

1935 Walter Williams dies, Frederick Middlebush becomes university president, and Don Faurot becomes Tiger football coach.

1937 The city purchases the Allton airfield and in 1938 holds an airshow to dedicate the $250,000 Municipal Airport.

1938 With the help of the WPA, Columbia builds a National Guard Armory.

1939 In June Columbia inaugurates bus service with a fare of a nickel a ride.

1940 A Civilian Conservation Corps camp is established near West Boulevard and Worley Street ● The state completes Columbia's Ellis Fischel State Cancer Hospital.

1945 The university's board of curators approves reestablishment of a four-year medical school on July 27.

1949 On March 29 Columbians approve a new city charter instituting a manager/council form of government.

1952 Ozark Airlines gives Columbia its first regularly scheduled airline passenger service.

1953 On December 21 television station KOMU begins broadcasting in Columbia.

1962 Stephens becomes a four-year college with the accreditation of its B.F.A.-degree program.

1967 Segregated public education ends with the closing of the Douglass elementary program.

1969 Christian College becomes Columbia College.

1973 Rock Bridge High School opens.

1974 Columbia Regional Hospital opens ● Francis Quadrangle on the university campus is placed on the National Register of Historic Places.

1978 The Missouri, Kansas & Texas Railroad abandons the 80-year-old branch line that served Columbia from McBain.

COLUMBIA BUILDINGS ON THE NATIONAL REGISTER

"Blind" Boone home, Fourth Street between Broadway & Walnut

Sanford F. Conley house, 602 Sanford Place

Frederick Douglass School, 310 North Providence Road

Francis Quadrangle Historic District (Red Campus), University of Missouri-Columbia

David Gordon house and Collins log cabin, 2100 East Broadway (Stephens Lake Property)

Greenwood Heights, 3005 Mexico Gravel Road

Maplewood, Nifong Boulevard and Ponderosa Drive

Missouri, Kansas & Texas Railroad Depot, 402 East Broadway

Missouri State Teachers Association, 407 South Sixth Street

Missouri Theater, 203 South Ninth Street

Missouri United Methodist Church, 204 South Ninth Street

Pierce Pennant Motor Hotel (Candlelight Lodge), 1406 Old Highway 40 West

St. Paul's A.M.E. Church, 501 Park Street

Second Baptist Church, 407 East Broadway

Second Christian Church, 401 North Fifth Street

Senior Hall, Stephens College campus

Tiger Hotel, 23 South Eighth Street

Wabash Railroad Station and Freight House, 126 North Tenth Street

NON-STRUCTURAL SITES ON THE REGISTER

Gordon Tract Archaeological Site, Hinkson Creek

Sanborn Field and Soil Erosion Plots, University of Missouri-Columbia

SUGGESTED READING

Atherton, Lewis E. *The Frontier Merchant in Mid-America.* University of Missouri Studies, LV. Columbia: University of Missouri Press, 1971.

_____ . "Life, Labor and Society in Boone County, Missouri As Revealed in the Correspondance of an Immigrant Slave Owning Family From North Carolina." *Missouri Historical Review* 38 (1944): 277-304, 408-429.

Batterson, Paulina Ann. *The First Forty Years: A Brief History of Columbia, Missouri, Prior To 1860.* Columbia: Columbia Chamber of Commerce, 1965.

"Boone County Courthouses: A Pictorial Feature." *Missouri Historical Review* 51 (1956): 97-98.

Brownlee, Richard S.; Goodrich, James W.; and Dains, Mary K. "The State Historical Society of Missouri, 1898-1973: A Brief History." *Missouri Historical Review* 68 (1973): 1-27.

Bryant, Keith L. "George Caleb Bingham: The Artist As A Whig Politician." *Missouri Historical Review* 59 (1965): 448-463.

Christ-Janer, Albert. *George Caleb Bingham of Missouri.* New York: Dodd, 1940.

Clayton, Charles C. "Walter Williams: Weekly Newspaper Editor." *Missouri Historical Review* 58 (1964): 1818-421.

Columbia Missouri Herald, 25th Anniversary Historical Edition. Columbia: Press of E.W. Stephens, 1895.

Committee on Historic Sites and Tours of the Columbia-Boone County Sesqui-centennial Commission. *A Boone County Album.* Columbia: Kelly Press, 1971.

Crighton, John C. "The Columbia Female Academy: A Pioneer in Education for Women." *Missouri Historical Review* 64 (1970): 177-196.

_____ . *A History of Columbia and Boone County,* a series of 141 articles which appeared in the *Columbia Daily Tribune* between June 25, 1972, and March 20, 1977.

_____ . "Robert Beverly Price II: Banker and Philanthropist." *Missouri Historical Review* 70 (1976): 306-314.

_____ . *Stephens: A Story of Educational Innovation.* Columbia: The American Press, 1970.

Crisler, Robert M. "Missouri's 'Little Dixie.' " *Missouri Historical Review* 42 (1948): 130-139.

Curtis, Winterton Conway. "A Damned Yankee Professor in Little Dixie: Abstracts from the Autobiographical Notes of Winterton C. Curtis." *Columbia Missourian,* April 2-20, 1957.

Dains, Mary K. "University of Missouri Football: The First Decade." *Missouri Historical Review* 70 (1975): 20-54.

Demos, John. "George Caleb Bingham: The Artist As Social Historian." *American Quarterly* 17 (1965): 218-228.

Deutch, Miriam, ed. *Images From Columbia's Past, 1865-1945.* Columbia: Waters Publishing Company, 1982.

Dictionary of American Biography contains sketches of Columbians: Maude Adams, George Caleb Bingham, Philemon Bliss, Charles Henry Hardin, William Andrew Hirth, Richard Henry Jesse, James Sidney Rollins, Edwin William Stephens, William Franklin Switzler, Walter Williams.

Doherty, Paul C. "The Columbia-Providence Plank Road." *Missouri Historical Review* 57 (1962): 53-69.

Duffner, Robert W. "Slavery in Missouri River Counties, 1820-1865." Ph.D. dissertation, University of Missouri-Columbia, 1974.

East, Wilbur D. "A Descriptive Survey of the Negro Churches in Columbia." Master's thesis, University of Missouri, 1938.

Flynn, Timothy Clark. "Missouri of the *Columbia Missourian.*" Master's thesis, University of Missouri-Columbia, 1973.

Fuell, Melissa. *Blind Boone: His Early Life and his Achievements.* Kansas City: Burton Publishing Co., 1915.

Gafke, Roger A. *A History of Public School Education in Columbia.* Columbia: Public School District, 1978.

Gates, Paul W. "The Railroads of Missouri, 1850-1870." *Missouri Historical Review* 26 (1932): 126-141.

Gentry, North Todd. *The Bench and Bar of Boone County, Missouri.* Columbia: North Todd Gentry, 1916.

_____ . "Legal and Illegal Sales of Liquor in Boone County." *Missouri Historical Review* 28 (1934): 173-183.

_____ . *One Hundred Years' History of Columbia Presbyterian Church.*

_____ . Columbia: North Todd Gentry, 1928.

_____ . "Proposed Railroads in Northeast Missouri." *Missouri Historical Review* 26 (1932): 368-373.

Gerhard, Ralph Edward. "A History of Calvary Episcopal Church in Columbia, Missouri, 1855-1955." Master's thesis, University of Missouri, 1955.

Grenz, Suzanna M. *The Black Community In Boone County, Missouri, 1850-1900.* Ph.D. dissertation, University of Missouri-Columbia, 1979.

Hale, Allean (Lemmon). *Petticoat Pioneer: The Story of Christian College, Oldest College for Women West of the Mississippi.* Revised ed. St. Paul: North Central Publishing Co., 1968.

Hall, Elizabeth Dorsett. "William Franklin Switzler: Editor, Politician, and Humanitarian." Master's thesis, University of Missouri, 1951.

Kantor, Harvey A. "The Barth Family: A Case Study of Pioneer Immigrant Merchants." *Missouri Historical Review* 62 (1968): 410-430.

Lander, Byron G. "The Making of Missouri's Equal Pay Law (1983) and the Legislative Process." *Missouri Historical Review* 77 (1983): 310-327.

Lemmer, George F. "The Early Agricultural Fairs of Missouri." *Agricultural History* 17 (1943): 145-152.

_____ . "Early Leaders in Livestock Improvement in Missouri." *Missouri Historical Review* 37 (1942): 29-39.

McDermott, John Francis. *George Caleb Bingham, River Portraitist.* Norman: University of Oklahoma Press, 1959.

McGettigan, James William, Jr. "Boone County Slaves: Sales, Estate Divisions and Families, 1820-1865." *Missouri Historical Review* 72 (1978): 176-197, 271-295.

The Making of the Black Community in Columbia. Mayor's Steering Committee to Commemorate the Contribution of Black Columbians, 1981.

Mering, John. "The Political Transition of James S. Rollins." *Missouri Historical Review* 53 (1959): 217-226.

Moss, James E., ed. "A Missouri Confederate in the Civil War: The Journal of Henry Martyn Cheavens, 1862-1863." *Missouri Historical Review* 57 (1962): 16-52.

Pendergast, Beth. "Smithton, Missouri." *Missouri Historical Review* 70 (1976): 134-141.

Pike, Francis, et al. *One Hundred Years, Sacred Heart Parish, Columbia, Missouri, 1881-1981.* Columbia: Sacred Heart Parish, 1981.

Pike, Leslie Francis. *Ed Watson—Country Editor: His Life And Times.* Marceline, Missouri: Walsworth Publishing Co., 1982.

Priddy, Bob. "Across Our Wide Missouri: Jane Froman 'With A Song In Her Heart.'" *Missouri Life,* July-August, 1980.

Quinn, Constantz. "History of Intercollegiate Athletics, University of Missouri." Master's thesis, University of Missouri, 1948.

Rollins, C.B., ed. "Letters of George Caleb Bingham to James S. Rollins." *Missouri Historical Review* 32 (1937-1938): 3-34, 164-202, 340-377, 484-522. 33 (1938-1939): 45-78, 203-299, 349-384, 499-526.

Saloutos, Theodore. "William Hirth and the Missouri Farmers' Association." *Missouri Historical Review* 44 (1949): 1-20.

Smith, Joe E. "Early Movies and Their Impact on Columbia." *Missouri Historical Review* 74 (1979): 72-85.

Stephens, E.W. "The Missouri Intelligencer and Boon's Lick Advertiser." *Missouri Historical Review* 13 (1919): 361-371.

Stephens, Frank Fletcher. *History of the Missouri Methodist Church of Columbia, Missouri.* Nashville, Tennessee, 1965.

———. *A History of the University of Missouri.* Columbia: University of Missouri Press, 1962.

Switzler, William F. *History of Boone County, Missouri.* St. Louis: Western Historical Co., 1882.

Thomas, David Morley. *History of Missouri University Football, 1890-1962.* Master's thesis, University of Missouri, 1964.

Voss, Stuart F. "Town Growth in Central Missouri, 1815-1880: An Urban Chaparral." *Missouri Historical Review* 64 (1969-1970): 64-80, 197-217, 322-350.

Viles, Jonas. *The University of Missouri: A Centennial History.* Columbia: University of Missouri, 1939.

Welsh, Donald H. "Travel By Stage on the Boonslick Road." *Missouri Historical Review* 54 (1960): 335-340.

Williams, Sara Lockwood. "A Study of the *Columbia Missouri Herald* from 1889 to 1908." Master's thesis, University of Missouri, 1931.

PATRONS

The following individuals, companies, and organizations have made a valuable commitment to the quality of this publication. Windsor Publications and the Columbia Chamber of Commerce gratefully acknowledge their participation in *From Southern Village to Midwestern City: Columbia, An Illustrated History.*

Aardvarx
Dr. and Mrs. T.R. Anderson
John Patrick Barnes
Barth's Clothing Co., Inc.*
Boone County Lumber Company*
Boone Hospital Center*
Boone Tavern & Restaurant
Brady's Columbia Glass & Paint Co.
The Brass Crow, Ltd.
Dr. and Mrs. Roger Bumgarner
Cal-Type Office Systems
Cancer Research Center

Cleek's Appliance and Carpet*
Columbia-Boone County League of
    Women Voters
Columbia Clearing House
    Association*
Columbia College*
Columbia Daily Tribune *
Columbia Insurance Companies*
Columbia Public School District*
Credit Bureau of Columbia*
Engineering Surveys and Services
John Epple Construction Company*
Robert E. Frazier, M.D.
General Telephone Company of the
    Midwest
Larry and Jan Grossman
Bob and Cookie Hagan
KCBJ-TV
Kelly Press, Inc.*
Kentucky Fried Chicken
KFRU Radio Station*
Knipp Construction Company*

KOMU-TV, ABC Affiliate
Los Bandidos
McDonald's Restaurants of Columbia
MFA Incorporated*
Mid-Missouri Mental Health Center*
Mid-State Distributing Co.*
Miller Dental Associates, Inc.
Missouri Store Company*
The A.F. Neate Dry Goods Co.*
John Neuffer & Associates
OATS, Incorporated
Pepsi-Cola Bottling Co. of Columbia,
    Inc.
Riback Supply Company, Inc.*
Mr. and Mrs. David B. Rogers
Dr. and Mrs. Garth S. Russell
Seams to Me
Shelter Insurance Companies*
Silvey Corporation*
Rodney and Alberta Smith
Stephens College*
Horace E. Thomas, M.D.
Tiger Hotel*
University of Missouri-Columbia
Vickers, Inc.
Dick and Joyce Walls
Wayland Office Products
Williams-Keepers, CPAs

*Partners in Progress of *From Southern Village to Midwestern City: Columbia, An Illustrated History.* The histories of these companies and organizations appear in Chapter Seven, beginning on page 93.

This University of Missouri faculty meeting, photographed circa 1890, probably took place in a room in the original Academic Hall. The only woman present was Mrs. Royal, "chaperon of women students." The ninth man, counting from the left, is professor of chemistry Paul Schweitzer, a nationally recognized teacher and scholar in his own day, and one whose name identifies a university building today. SHSM

INDEX

Partners in Progress Index

Barth's Clothing Co., Inc., 112-113
Boone County Lumber Company, 111
Boone Hospital Center, 96, 97
Cleek's Appliance and Carpet, 124
Columbia Chamber of Commerce, 94
Columbia Clearing House Association, 118, 119
Columbia College, 98
Columbia Daily Tribune, 107
Columbia Insurance Companies, 110
Columbia Public School District, 125
Credit Bureau of Columbia, 115
Epple Construction Company, John, 95
Kelly Press, Inc., 116
KFRU Radio Station, 114
Knipp Construction Company, 104, 106
MFA Incorporated, 102-103
Mid-Missouri Mental Health Center, 122, 123
Mid-State Distributing Co., 117
Missouri Store Company, 108, 109
Neate Dry Goods Co., The A.F., 121
Riback Supply Company, Inc., 120
Shelter Insurance Companies, 99
Silvey Corporation, 100, 101
Stephens College, 126
Tiger Hotel, 127

General Index
Italicized numbers indicate illustrations.

A
Academic Hall, 33, 48, 77, 85, *132, 133*
Adams, Maud, 68, 69
Addams, Jane, 30
Agriculture, 36, 38, 43
Anderson, William C. "Bloody Bill," *22*, 25
Allton, John, 37
Arnold, Thomas A., 58
Aslin, Neil, 76
Athenaean Society, 70
Athens Hotel, 27
"Athens of Missouri," 45
Atherton, Lewis, 80
Audrain County, 16
Automobiles, 37

B
Balsamo, Frank, Sr., 56
Banking, 39
Banks, Hartley H., 41
Baptist College, 48, 51, 68, 69
Baptist Female College, 47
Baptist religion, 61, 62
Barrie, J.M., 69
Barth, Joseph, 13
Barth, Moses, 35
Barth, Victor, *13*
Bass, Eli, 48
Batterson, Paulina Ann, 80
Battle of Boonville, 22
Battle of Westport, 25
Bennett, James H., 39, 47
Benton, Thomas Hart, 23
Biggs, Mary Brady, *54, 55*

Bihr, Frederick, 13
Bingham, Clara, 68, 69
Bingham, George Caleb, 26, 67, *83*
Black Hawk Indian War, 21
Boon's Lick, 9, 10
Boon's Lick Trail, 25, *76, 77, 78*
Boone, Daniel, 9, *10*, 67
Boone, John W. "Blind," 11, 12, 63, 66, 67, 77
Boone County Agricultural Society, 38
Boone County Colored Agricultural and Mechanical Association, 38
Boone County Council of Defense, 27
Boone County Court, 62
Boone County Courthouse, 9, 10, 25, 30, *31, 32*, 70, 92
Boone County Fair, 38, *40*
Boone County Ham, 40
Boone County Historical Society, 80, 86
Boone County Home Mutual Fire Insurance Company, 39
Boone County Hospital, 41, 80
Boone County Medical Society, 58
Boone County Mill, *82, 83*
Boone County National Bank, 39
Boone Guards, 21
Boyle, Charley, 11, 13
Brewer Field House, *40, 41*, 71
Broadway (theater), 73
Brownlee, Richard S., 80
Bryan, William Jennings, 24, 25, 26, *74, 75*
Buchroeders Jewelers, 39

C
Calvary Episcopal Church, 62
Campbell, Alexander, 61
Canvassing for a Vote (painting), 83
Capen House, 10, 86, *87*
Caulfield, Henry S., 58
Cave, William, 22
Cemetery Hill, 19
Central Bank, 39
Cheavens, Henry Martyn, *23*
Chicago Art Institute, 80
Chisholm, Shirley, *30*
Christian College, 11, 12, 13, 36, 45, 47, 48, *49, 50*, 51, 55, 56, *57*, 58, 59, *59*, 61, 62, 70, 73, 80, *136*
Christian College Club, 58
Christian religion, 61, 62
Civil Rights Movement, 27
Civil War, 11, 13, 21, 23, 25, 26, 27, 48, 51, 55, 62, 89
Clark, William, 9
College of Agriculture, 47, 58
College of Engineering, 66
College of Medicine, 58
College of Normal Instruction, 58
"Collegetown, U.S.A.," 45
Columbia Automobile Company, 37
Columbia Baptist Church, 62
Columbia Baptist Female College, 47
Columbia Board of Education, 39
Columbia Board of Trustees, 22
Columbia Cemetery Association, 84
Columbia Chamber of Commerce, 41, 70
Columbia Club, 64
Columbia College, 45, 47, 80
Columbia College of Music and Oratory, 12
Columbia Country Club, 39, 73
Columbia Daily Tribune (newspaper), 58

Columbia Equal Suffrage Association, 27, 30
Columbia Female Academy, 10, 13, 45, 47, 59
Columbia Fire Department, *32, 33*, 78
Columbia Gas Company, *34, 35*
Columbia Greys, 22
Columbia Hall, 55
Columbia Lyceum, 66, 67
Columbia Missourian (newspaper), 58
Columbia Missouri Herald (newspaper), 58
Columbia Opera House, 75
Columbia Presbyterian Female Sewing Society, 63
Columbia Public Schools, 88
Columbia Temperance Society, 67
Columbia Theater, *18*, 64, 73
Columbia Tigers, 25
Columbia Water and Light Company, 33
Comfort, S.W., 39
Commercial Club, 33, 39, 41, 43
Committee to Commemorate the Contributions of Black Columbians, 80
Congregations of the Church of God, 62
Construction, 10, 12
Cosmopolitan Club, 73
County Election, The (painting), 67
Cox, Lester E., 37
Crighton, John C., 80
Crowder, Enoch, 29
Crowder Hall, *46*
Cummings, Charles E., 51
Cummings Academy, 11, 51
Curtis, C.W., 76
Curtis, Winterton C., 75

D
Daniel Boone Tavern, 55
David H. Hickman High School, *18*, 55, 84
Davis, Jefferson, 22
Disciples of Christ, 61, 62
Disciples of Christ (Christian) Church, 47, 61, 62
Distillery, 36
Dobbs, Ella Victoria, 30, 57
Doniphan, Alexander, 21
Douglass Pool, 73
Douglass School, 19, 51, *54*, 55
Drug Shop, The, 36, *37*
Duncan, William H., 39
Dye, William E., 27

E
Eagle's Nest, 77
Eisenhower, Dwight D., 26
Elite Theater, 73
Ellis, Elmer, 80
Ellis Fischel State Cancer Hospital, 41
Ellis Library, 72, 88
English, William Francis, 80
Entertainment, 38
Every Saturday (magazine), 46, 47
Exchange National Bank, 39
Excelsior School, 51

F
Fairgrounds, 4, 6, *18*
Farm Club, 38
Farmer's Fair, *50*
Farmers Week, 36, *37*
Field School, 76
Fifth Missouri Regiment, *28, 29*

134